THE USBORNE BOOK OF
THE FUTURE
A TRIP IN TIME TO THE YEAR 2000 AND BEYOND

KENNETH GATLAND & DAVID JEFFERIS

THE USBORNE BOOK OF
THE FUTURE

CONTENTS

PART ONE
ROBOTS
SCIENCE & MEDICINE INTO THE 21st CENTURY

Robot explorers

Already, automatic spaceprobes have landed on, or flown by, most of the planets in the Solar System. In the future, robot exploration teams like the one shown here could prepare the way for humans to follow. In this picture a group of robots is erecting the domes of a planetary base. By the time the human explorers arrive, their quarters will be warmed and ready to live in.

To the right, you can see a three-legged robot of a type which might be used for long-range reconnaissance.

PART ONE

ROBOTS

SCIENCE & MEDICINE INTO THE 21st CENTURY

INTRODUCTION

In the first section of this book, you can see some of the ideas which scientists are suggesting as ways to solve problems such as the energy crisis and global pollution.

Robots, which form the central theme, will help mankind run an increasingly complex world. Few of these machines, using advanced computers systems as their 'brains' will look like the popular image of a robot, a machine in the shape of a person. The real robtos will come in all shapes and sizes, according to the job they are designed for. An arithmetic robot of today, for example, does not look like a maths teacher – it is small, rectangular and its 'face' has buttons on. It is called an electronic calculator.

The word 'robot' comes from the Czech word 'robota' meaning 'labour'. The name was used in a 1920 play called R.U.R. – Rossum's Universal Robots, in which mass-produced robots in human form turn on their creators and exterminate them.

Since then, many stories have been written about warlike robots. If you count the guidance computers aboard nuclear missiles as simple robots, then those stories have, in part, come true.

FROM STONE-AGE TOOLS TO SPACE-AGE COMPUTERS

The history of man has been that of a curious animal learning about the world and changing it to suit itself.

On these pages you can see some of the major inventions that have enabled mankind to become the dominant species on Planet Earth.

With the invention of the atomic bomb, it has become possible for a major war to cause a complete collapse of world-wide civilization.

Let us hope that enough people remember that our ape ancestors first succeeded by co-operating with each other. The lesson should not be forgotten, otherwise there may be no future worth writing or reading about.

1 Man the toolmaker

The discovery that useful tools like knives and axes could be made by chipping stones and flints dates back at least 250,000 years. Tools like these were not only used for hunting and skinning animals – they were valuable and were used for trading.

2 The dawn of agriculture

Agriculture was the main way in which primitive man developed toward civilization. Instead of being hunters and nomads, people could settle and build houses, villages and cities. The plough was first used about 5,000 BC. Ones like the type shown are still used in parts of the Middle East.

3 The birth of science

The foundations of modern science were laid in Ancient Greece during the 500 years before the birth of Christ. The steam turbine shown here was invented a little later by an engineer called Hero, born about 20 AD. When water boiled in the sphere, the escaping steam spun it round on its axle.

4 The invention of gunpowder

The Chinese invented this explosive mixture, using it for rockets and fire arrows as early as 700 AD. It was not used in Europe until five centuries later. The first recorded use of a gun was in the town of Amberg in 1301 and a brass cannon was used at the siege of Metz 23 years later.

5 Observing the invisible

Dutch spectacle maker Zacharias Jansen invented the microscope about 1590. He saw a microscopic world which no-one had known existed. In 1608, another Dutchman, Hans Lippershey, invented the telescope. Galileo Galilei later became famous for his astronomical discoveries using the new invention.

6 Surgery and medicine

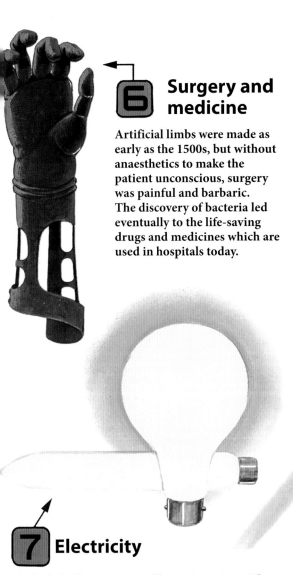

Artificial limbs were made as early as the 1500s, but without anaesthetics to make the patient unconscious, surgery was painful and barbaric. The discovery of bacteria led eventually to the life-saving drugs and medicines which are used in hospitals today.

8 The atomic age

The threat of atomic war has hung over the peoples of the world ever since two bombs were exploded over Hiroshima and Nagasaki in 1945, ending World War II. In 1952, the hydrogen bomb was first exploded. It used the fusion nuclear reaction which powers the Sun. Yet the same power, controlled, could provide cheap and safe electric power.

7 Electricity

The light bulb was invented by an American, Thomas Edison, in 1878. This, together with other 19th-century electrical inventions such as the dynamo and motor, changed the world and led to electronic devices like TV and radio. Most homes now have more than 50 electrical devices in them – try counting the ones in your own home.

9 Tele-communications

150 years ago, it took weeks for a message to get from Europe to the USA. Now it takes less than a second using electronic equipment like radio and television. Using the same electronic principles, radar beams sweep the skies, providing an almost instantaneous check on everything in them from storm clouds to atom bombers.

10 Computers

The first electronic computer was called ENIAC and was completed in 1943. Today's transistorized computers are used in everything from cameras to watches. Though only a super-fast adding machine, the computer has some similarities to the human brain and some people think that the computer will eventually far exceed the brain's capacity.

Now read on... into the fantastic world of the future...

PROVIDING FOR A POWER-HUNGRY PLANET

Plentiful energy is the basis of world civilization and future supplies are essential.

At present, oil is used for most energy needs, but supplies are limited, so new sources of energy have to be found.

On these pages, you can see some of the ways in which energy, in the form of electricity, might be generated in the 21st century.

Power from the waves

Salter's Ducks, named after their Scottish inventor Stephen Salter, are teardrop-shaped pods which move up and down in ocean waves like nodding ducks. As they nod, pumps inside them move up and down too, driving power-producing generators.

Prototypes are already being built, and eventually long lines of them may surround the world's coastlines.

The picture shows one of the more hazardous aspects of this non-polluting power source. Engineers struggle to replace a damaged pump unit during a howling North Atlantic gale. Critics of the ducks say that long lines of them would be a hazard to shipping. Also they would affect, perhaps badly, tide and wave patterns.

Nuclear fusion

At present, this is the most likely oil replacement. Various types of fusion reactor are under development. The one shown uses laser beams to crush a pellet of deuterium. They crush it until its atoms fuse together – giving off immense heat in the process. The heat is used to turn water to steam, which then spins electric turbines to generate electricity.

An advantage of nuclear fusion is that it produces little radioactive waste unlike present-day fission reactors, some of whose wastes will take centuries before becoming safe. Also, its fuel, deuterium, comes from seawater which is available free and in vast quantities.

Power from the ocean depths

On the left engineers carry out a repair operation on a giant power station of the future. It uses the difference in temperature between warm surface waters and cool deep waters to generate power.

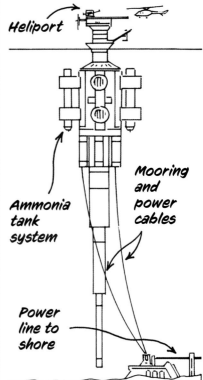

Heliport

Ammonia tank system

Mooring and power cables

Power line to shore

How it works

At the station's core is an ammonia tank. Ammonia needs only a small temperature change to turn from a liquid to a gas and back again.

Warm surface water is pumped around the ammonia tank. As the ammonia warms up it turns into gas. The gas is piped to a turbine, spinning it to generate electricity. Cold water is pumped up from the depths to cool the ammonia, turning it back to a liquid, ready to repeat the cycle once more.

The energy outlook

Energy will be generated by a wide variety of methods in the 21st century. It will be an almost totally electric world, with liquid hydrogen replacing oil as a fuel to power, for example, aircraft and cars.

ENERGY FROM SPACE

The development of solar cells, flat panes of silicon material which convert the energy contained in sunlight to electricity, has enabled scientists to dream up the 'power station in space' idea.

Using solar cells to supply electricity is possible here on Earth – calculators, watches and battery chargers are some of the gadgets now on sale powered by them. The problem is that on very cloudy days and at night the cells do not receive much light, so can supply little or no electricity.

In space, there is a continuous torrent of sunpower, ready for use by the power station in space.

1

▲ This dumpy-looking spaceship is the Boeing aircraft company's idea of a Heavy Lift Vehicle of the 1990s. With a mighty roar the HLV takes off, loaded with up to 227 tonnes of cargo. Its destination, a 'building site' in orbit.

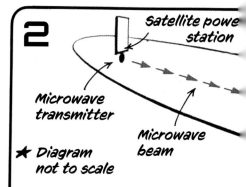

2

Satellite power station

Microwave transmitter

★ Diagram not to scale

Microwave beam

The HLV's cargo is helping to build the Satellite Solar Power Station, shown in diagram form above and in the big picture below. The SSPS orbits Earth in almost continuous sunshine. The electricity supplied by its vast panel

The Solar cycle

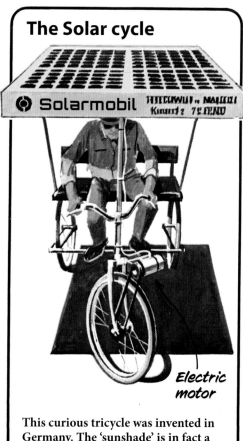

Solarmobil

Electric motor

This curious tricycle was invented in Germany. The 'sunshade' is in fact a solar-cell panel which powers a small electric motor near the front wheel.

The motor is powerful enough to keep the Solarmobile rolling along on flat roads. Up hills the rider has to help by pedalling and on cloudy days or at night the Solarmobile stays at home as its solar cells do not generate power in the dark.

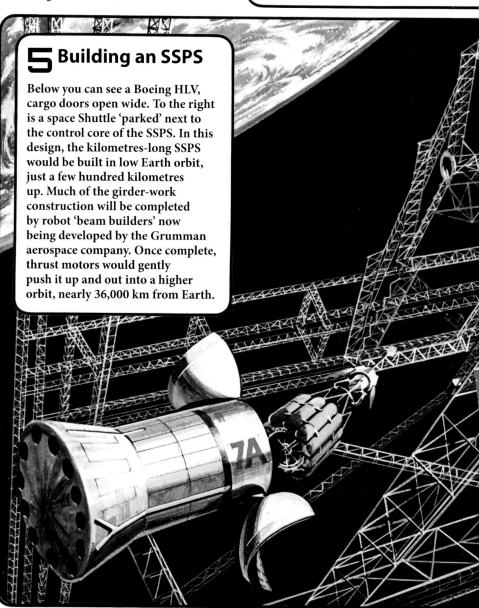

5 ## Building an SSPS

Below you can see a Boeing HLV, cargo doors open wide. To the right is a space Shuttle 'parked' next to the control core of the SSPS. In this design, the kilometres-long SSPS would be built in low Earth orbit, just a few hundred kilometres up. Much of the girder-work construction will be completed by robot 'beam builders' now being developed by the Grumman aerospace company. Once complete, thrust motors would gently push it up and out into a higher orbit, nearly 36,000 km from Earth.

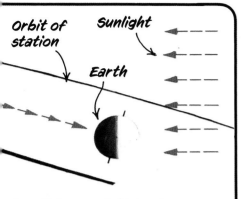

Orbit of station

Sunlight

Earth

...solar cells is converted into microwave ...ergy (like a super power radar beam) ...ich is aimed at a receiving station on ...rth. The SSPS is in 'geostationary' ...bit – one which keeps over the same ...ot on Earth.

▲ The HLV returns to its Earth base after dumping its cargo in orbit. The landing 'pad' is a giant circular lake on which the HLV splashes down. (It will be designed to float.) After refuelling it will be re-furbished, then will fly again.

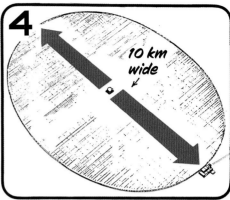

10 km wide

▲ This is the 10 km-wide receiving aerial for the SSPS's microwave beam. At the bottom right you can see the station which converts the microwaves back into electricity, ready to supply the world's power needs.

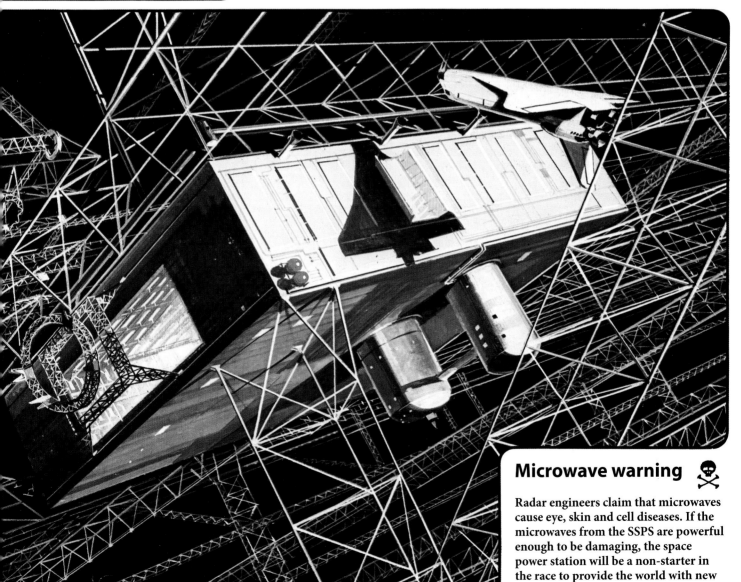

Microwave warning ☠

Radar engineers claim that microwaves cause eye, skin and cell diseases. If the microwaves from the SSPS are powerful enough to be damaging, the space power station will be a non-starter in the race to provide the world with new energy sources.

9

FACTORIES IN ORBIT

The First Industrial Revolution began in England in the 18th century, introducing powered machinery to replace human and animal muscle power.

The Second Industrial Revolution, still going on, began in the USA early this century, replacing human brain-power with automatic control devices, such as computers.

The Third Industrial Revolution has yet to happen. It will be the moving of many industrial operations (particularly polluting ones) away from Earth and into space.

Is this imagination? Many experts think not – their only arguments are about when, not if, it will happen.

Why make things in space?

The secret of making things in space is that materials float weightless, a condition impossible to achieve on Earth. Materials of great purity melted inside space furnaces can be made free of contact with containers. They include new alloys which will not mix on Earth and foam steels so light they will float on water. Space factories also have direct access to a vacuum – necessary for many industrial processes – and the free energy of sunlight.

Key to Vulcan One, the space factory of the future

Vulcan One, orbiting high above the Earth's surface, is named after the Roman god of metalworkers and fire. The factory is a prototype for other larger ones still in the planning stages back on Earth.

1. A Space Shuttle, doors open, has just been loaded with a module full of space-made (the best) optical glass for use in high quality instruments. By the time Vulcan One is in service, the Shuttle, built several years earlier, will be well used indeed and showing signs of wear and tear. Aerospace engineers will no doubt be planning a replacement.
2. Vulcan One is a unit structure. Each module has been ferried up in the cargo hold of a Shuttle.
3. The command module contains approach radars and control equipment.
4. Solar panels supply power for the factory. Their angle and power output is controlled by the command module.
5. The Earth. Once the Third Industrial Revolution is underway, the pressures on its ecological balance from polluting heavy industry should be eased.
6. Manufacturing modules are plugged into the factory's spine as required. Each one makes a different product.
7. Service engineers keep the factory operating efficiently.
8. Vulcan Two, slightly larger and slightly more advanced, pointing the way to the huge factories of the 1990s and 21st century.
9. Storing finished products is no problem – they are stored in sealed cans in space, anchored with elastic netting.

Some products from Vulcan One

These three products are ones which can be made in space using present-day knowledge. Others will no doubt be developed. Shown below is the equipment used to make urokinase, a medicine for treating unwanted blood clots, which if free in the blood-stream can disable or kill.

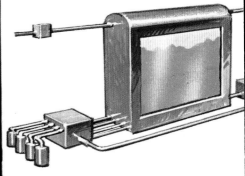

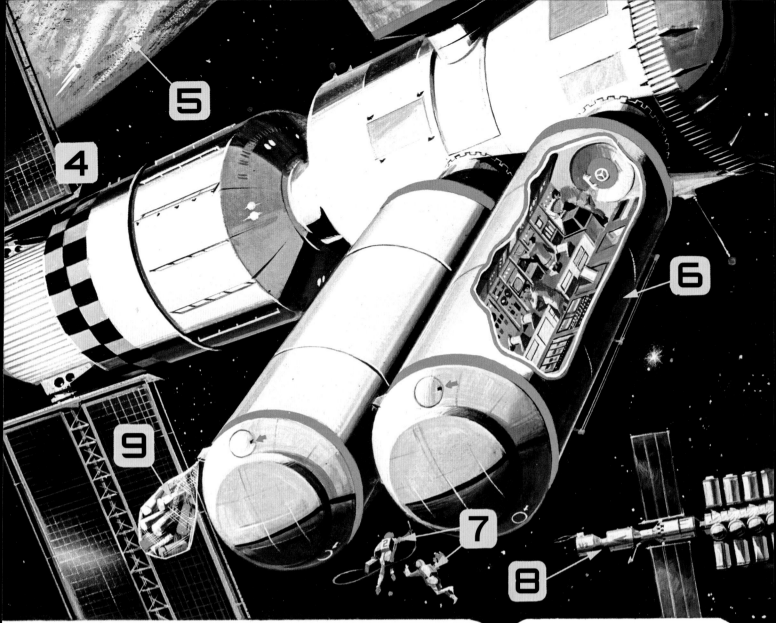

This is the front fan of a jumbo jet engine. Space-made fan blades would be stronger than those made on Earth and could withstand super-high temperatures allowing engines using them to operate very efficiently. One estimate of the fuel saved if space-made blades were used on airliners is an amazing 4,000 million litres a year.

Crystals used in electronic equipment can be grown large and pure in orbit. The one photographed above was grown in Skylab, the American manned space laboratory, in 1974. The crystal's size and quality were a huge improvement over ones grown on Earth. Large-scale manufacturing of crystals in space ought to make them far cheaper to make than back on Earth, too.

A space oddity

At left is an earth-bound candle. Hot air rises over it. Fresh oxygen rushes in at the base keeping the wick burning. At right, the weightless space-candle burns with a globe-shaped flame. Hot air does not rise and in a few seconds the candle uses all the oxygen around it and seems to go out. But the heat can only escape by slowly radiating away, and if the candle is supplied with fresh oxygen later, it will mysteriously flare into life again.

GOLD MINES IN THE SKY

Many people foresee doom for technological civilization within the next century as a result of energy shortages, pollution problems and shortages of essential mineral resources.

You have already seen that there need be little reason for energy shortages. Dirty production processes can be taken 'off-planet' into orbit. And for natural resources, there is the mineral wealth of the entire Solar System.

Materials from the Moon, Asteroid Belt and Jupiter could be mined if it becomes necessary in the same way that rigs now drill for oil in the dangerous waters of the North Sea.

Moonminers

This picture shows two moonminers, supported aloft by compressed-gas powered backpacks. They carry electronic equipment designed for mineral surveying.

Down below are the two tracked vehicles they are using as a mobile base (the backpacks carry fuel for just a few minutes flight at a time), while on the right you can see the explosions set off in the lunar crust by other members of the survey team.

From recordings made of the explosions echoing through the lunar rock, the surveyors will be able to tell the composition of the rock in the area and whether it is of value in their quest for minerals.

Once a good site has been chosen, robot equipment will be installed to mine the minerals.

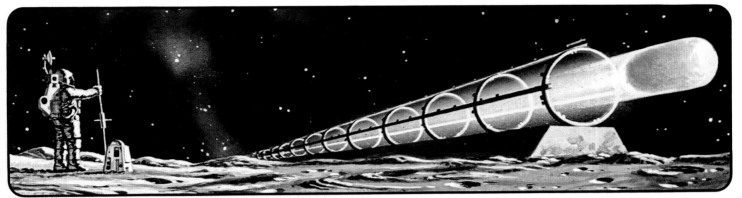

▲ There is no need for expensive rocket power to get materials (such as calcium and aluminium) off the Moon. This long machine does the job. It is an electromagnetic catapult, which accelerates mineral-carrying modules up to 2,400 metres a second, enough to escape the Moon's gravitational pull.

The modules would be aimed to finish their journeys close to space factories orbiting the Earth.

The catapult's foundations are made of moon-soil bulldozed into position. Power for the electromagnets is provided by solar cells. This base is near the Moon's South Pole where the Sun never sets, so the production of power is constant.

▲ Out in the Asteroid Belt, a prospector ship has a rich find – a kilometre-wide rock ball. When refined in a space factory orbiting Callisto, a moon of Jupiter, it should yield nearly 10 million tonnes of pure iron ore.

▲ An ion-drive engine and navigation system are installed on the rock. The low-thrust engine slowly eases the rock into a new orbit – one that will take it near Callisto, now the capital-world of human colonies in the outer Solar System.

▲ Months (or even years) later, the rock is met and slowed by an automatic collection tug, before being melted down and refined. A steady stream of asteroid rocks provides a constant supply of raw material, mainly iron and nickel, for factories.

▲ Jupiter is larger than all the other planets in the Solar System put together. Its atmosphere contains hydrogen, ammonia and other chemicals in vast quantities. Since Jupiter has no solid surface (its atmosphere just gets thicker and thicker as you go deeper) a hot-air balloon suspended in the upper atmosphere is the best way to mine the planet. Hung below the balloon are the refining and power plants necessary to 'sieve' the atmosphere of its chemical riches. Spacecraft like the one shown are used to carry the material up into space. The system would have to be completely automated – Jupiter has intense radiation belts too dangerous for humans to endure. Other hazards for the robots would include the storms raging in Jupiter's atmosphere.

LOOKING AFTER OUR WORLD

The best place to keep a watch over the Earth is from space. Satellites are already used to monitor Earth's vital natural resources and in the future their role will become even more varied and important.

'Eyes in space' can keep track of air and sea pollution and give advance warning of floods, drought and forest fires. By using special photographic equipment, pictures can show if crops are diseased or healthy.

There are thousands of man-made objects in orbit. Already space agencies have to plan carefully if they wish to put satellites into popular orbits. In the future, a rationing system may be set to avoid collisions.

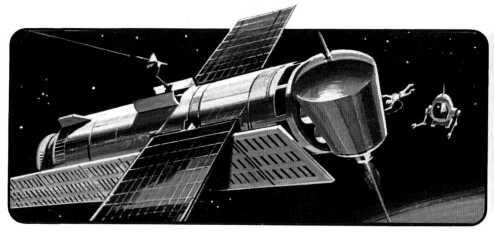

▲ This 14-tonne satellite, which could be in orbit by 1985, is designed to observe pollution and resources. It has two lasers – one above the solar cell 'wings' for communication with other satellites; the other, pointed downwards, is used to check the distance between the satellite and the Earth, enabling the satellite to detect, for example, changes in water level for flood detection and control. The laser distance-checker would be sensitive enough to detect changes of as little as 30 cm.

▲ Nearly 36,000 km above the equator, the Meteosat, put in orbit by the European Space Agency, provides a world weather watch. This picture, which shows Africa and South America, was taken on 9 December 1977. Satellites have provided the first means of reliable weather forecasting, even if only – at present – for very short periods ahead. In the future, long-range forecasting should become possible, though reliable ones of just a week ahead would make a good start.

▲ This satellite, shown being serviced by an astronaut-engineer, has a laser to measure the small movements in the Earth's crust which are early indicators of earthquakes. This one is focused on a reflector embedded in the ground near the

▲ Finding places where water may be found is vital in countries affected by drought and famine. Even present-day satellites like Landsat can detect underground water sources and places where crops can grow in desert areas.

▲ Satellites can detect clouds of locusts and other similar insects as they swarm from their breeding grounds. Early warning alerts help pest-control teams wipe out the insects (a locust is shown above) before they totally destroy the crop.

▲ These triangular satellites, each one 300 metres across, are in fact giant mirrors made of reflective aluminium foil. They are designed to focus sunlight onto the nightside of the world. The mirrors' beams could be switched from

▲ This colour picture shows fields of potatoes. Some of the crop has been affected by blight – diseased potatoes show up black. Satellite views can sometimes detect disease even before the farmer standing in his field.

▲ Forest fires cost thousands of millions of dollars a year in the USA alone. Satellites in orbit could detect and provide early warning of forests aflame. In this picture you can see a four-legged walking fire-fighting robot of the future attacking an

outbreak with fire-smothering chemicals. Machines like this, alerted by satellite, could reduce the cost – and danger to life and property – of forest fires. The walking design would enable the robot to fight fires in all sorts of awkward places.

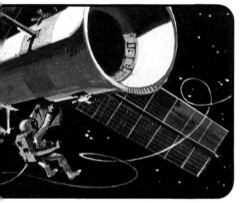

San Andreas fault in Southern California, USA. This zone, which has had major earthquakes before, is a prime candidate for a serious upheaval in the future. Early warnings provided by satellite could save thousands of lives and millions of dollars.

▲ Early warnings, provided by satellites like the one on the left, would enable rescue teams to move quickly into disaster areas. In this picture, a Red Cross hoverjet swoops low over a doomed city to pick up survivors as buildings rock and crumble.

The hoverjet is held aloft by four propellers, shrouded in circular ducts. For forward flight, the ducts swivel through 90 degrees to speed the craft to the nearest hospital. Its maximum speed would be about 450 kph.

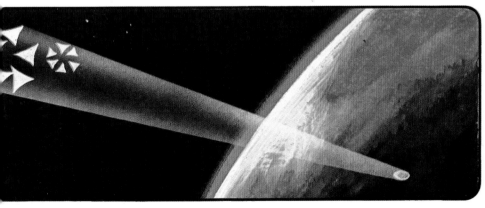

place to place, wherever light might be required. On the ground, the mirrors would look like bright stars. The light provided would be about 100 times that of the full moon on a clear night, or about the same as the light level between lamp

posts in a present-day city. Uses for such a system are varied. In a big power-failure, for example, they could be used to illuminate blacked-out towns and cities. They might be used to provide cheap lighting for major road junctions.

▲ This picture shows another use for space mirrors – illuminating fields for farmers to get the harvest in on time. As you can see, although there is enough light to work by, the sky remains completely dark with the stars out as usual.

FARMING ON LAND AND SEA

In 1900 the world's population was 1,550 million. By 2000, it will be rocketing over 6,000 million. The outlook for most of the peoples of the world is hunger or starvation unless food production keeps pace with the number of mouths to feed.

Research into improving soil, crops and animal breeds have produced striking advances in the past. Future improvements will need to avoid pollution through wrongly-used insecticides and soil erosion through over-cultivation.

▲ Meat will be expensive. You can already buy 'extenders' like this cheap soya-bean product. It is mixed into a meat stew to make it go further.

Superfarm, year 2020

Compared with a farm of the present-day, this one seems more like a factory. The high food production required by a vast human population may make factory farms the only way to avoid mass starvation.

1 Farmhouse. Weather reports arrive via satellite; computers keep track of stock and grain yields.
2 Automatic harvester glides along monorail tracks.
3 Helijet sprays fertilizer and weedkiller.
4 Grain is pumped along tubes to nearby city. Old-fashioned trucks are little-used.
5 Many people regard present-day factory farming of animals as cruel and unnecessary even though most are happy to buy cheap factory-farmed chickens. If people still want cheap meat, more of it may have to be produced in this way. Here, cattle are shown in space-saving multi-level pens.
6 Monorail train, loading up with beef.
7 Plastic domes protect crops like tomatoes and strawberries.
8 Orbiting space mirror provides night-lighting to boost crop yield.

Fish farming the underwater world

At present, man still gets food from the seas in an old-fashioned way – by hunting. This picture shows a better solution – a farm under the water.

1 Globe-shaped farmhouse, warm and dry, equipped with all the comforts of home, plus its own computer systems.
2 Pumping station draws up nutrients from the ocean depths for the fish cages.
3 Aqualung-equipped farmers are helped by dolphins, the sheepdogs of this underwater world. The nearest farmer has just fired a knockout dart at a stray shark. It will be towed away by a pair of dolphins.
4 Fish farm cage. The walls are made of air bubbles leaked from a pipe system. Fish stay behind the 'wall' as they dislike passing through the bubbles.
5 Farmers poke the suction hose of a fishing boat into a cage. The fish are sucked up into the boat to be gutted and fresh-frozen.

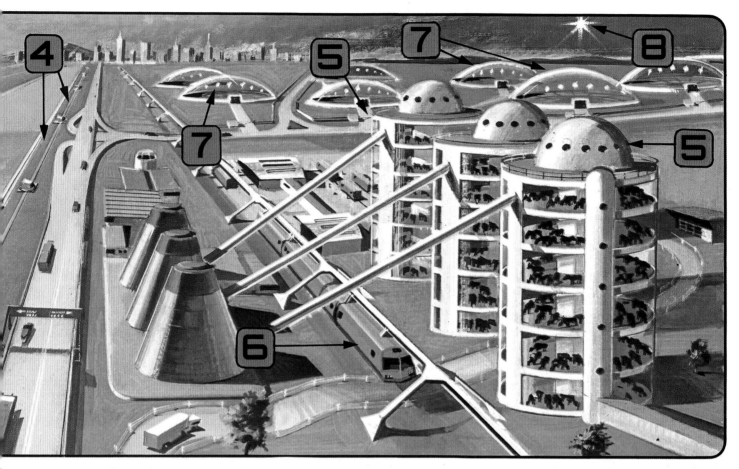

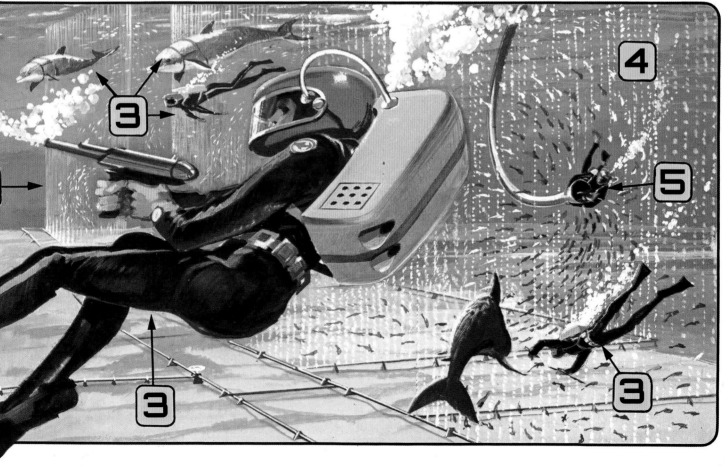

MEDICAL EMERGENCY

Despite advanced telephone and TV equipment and increased fuel prices, people are still going to travel from place to place in the future. The safety and reliability of transport systems is improving and will continue to improve, but no machine (or the person in charge of it) is perfect, or ever will be: accidents will happen.

On these pages you can see the sort of medical help that could be available to help an accident victim, in this case the burnt and broken-boned driver of a turbocar involved in a road smash.

Some of the medical aids are new, others are based on current researches.

1 Rescue services close in on the burning wreck of a turbine-engined car. As fire-fighting robots under the supervision of human firemen lay flame-quenching foam on the car, the nearest heli-ambulance descends to take care of the driver, still trapped. After he has been cut out of the wreck, he will be airlifted to hospital.

▲ The medics use a spraycan of 'synthetic skin' to treat severe burns. Like a person's own skin, the plastic film lets in air to help healing while keeping out bacteria, liquids and dirt. Material like this has already been developed.

▲ The patient is placed in a portable oxygen tent, and his condition is monitored by automatic sensor equipment. The results are radioed to the computer in the hospital awaiting them, providing an up-to-the-minute record of his condition.

The medics oversee the equipment and check all is well. The ambulance is a high-speed craft – once moving forward, its rotor blades slow, then stop to act as wings for fast flight. Flight-control is mainly by robot-pilot.

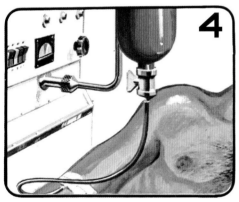

▲ Blood is always in short supply. In the future, artificial blood could be a possibility. Experiments in the USA as early as 1966 proved that 'fluorocarbon' liquids could be used, at least for short periods, to replace blood.

5 Preventive medicine, 21st century style

The emphasis in 21st-century medicine will be to prevent most illnesses from becoming serious in the first place, mainly by continuous medical checks from childhood, so that treatment can be administered as soon as any change is noted.

The advantage of this sort of medical treatment is that most people should need much less time in hospital and that medical money and equipment is freed for emergency cases like this one.

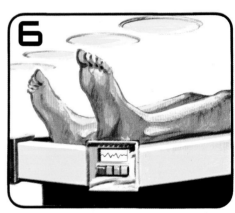

▲ In hospital, the burnt driver is placed on a hoverbed, which suspends him on a gentle cushion of air. As there is no pressure on burn areas, there is less pain and wounds heal more quickly. Dials control hover height and air temperature.

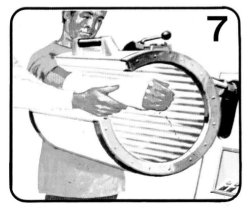

▲ Broken bones are set using plastic tape. It is half the weight of plaster of Paris, three times as strong, and waterproof. After wrapping, the tape is hardened by exposing it to an ultraviolet lamp like the cylindrical one shown above.

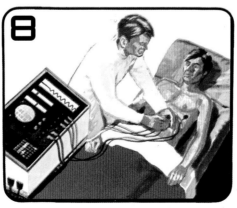

▲ In AD 46, a Roman doctor claimed to cure headaches using current from electric eels. American doctors have already updated the technique with some success. In the 21st century this cure might replace many drugs.

▲ The patient is returned home to familiar surroundings as soon as possible. Just in case of a relapse, he takes home a portable medical analyser which checks and automatically reports on his condition to the hospital computer.

PEOPLE OR MACHINES?

One of the most fantastic achievements of modern medicine has been the transplanting of organs (such as kidneys) from one person to another. Even more startling has been the invention of completely artificial replacements, or implants.

The silhouetted figure below shows the range of transplants and implants which could be put into a body, though it is very unlikely that one person would need them all. Most of the ones shown are already available. Some, such as the nuclear-powered heart have yet to be developed.

It might be possible to achieve near-immortality if organs were continually replaced as they wore out. There could be an unpleasant side-effect though – a black-market in replacement organs.

Exploring a heavy-gravity world in a powered exo-skeleton

This interplanetary explorer of the future has his strength boosted by his robot-like powered 'exo-skeleton'. Developed from present-day prototypes, the suit has a small nuclear reactor to give it the power it needs. Built-in sensors detect and boost the explorer's movements enabling him to walk on a heavy-gravity world (where he would be several times his Earth-weight), lift up large rock samples, and in an emergency run at up to 70 kph.

Key to the cyborg person

With more and more artificial organs available, tomorrow's people might be cyborgs – half human, half robots.

Certainly with the number of replacement organs shown here, the dividing line between man and machine is rather narrow. Parts marked * are not yet available, but soon will be.

1 Skull – made of animal bone
2 Cornea and lens of eye – plastic
3 Eyeball – plastic
4 Nose cartilage – silicone rubber
5 Shoulder joint – vitallium metal
6 Elbow joint – metal
7 Hip joint – a ceramic bone-like material called cerosium
8 Artery – dacron plastic tubing
9 Ear cartilage – silicone rubber
10 Jawbone – cerosium
11 Blood pressure regulator-electronic
12 Trachea (air passage)– silicone rubber
13 Lung – silicone rubber *
14 Heart – silicone rubber, nuclear powered *
15 Liver – transplant *
16 Kidney – transplant
17 Finger joints – metal
18 Bladder stimulator – electronic
19 Thighbone and knee joint – metal
20 Foot tendon – silicone rubber

ARTIFICIAL INTELLIGENCE

Many computer engineers are convinced that we are seeing the evolution of a new species – that of the intelligent machine.

Already chess-playing computers can beat all but a handful of human opponents. Although computers have to be programmed with instructions by people, it is possible to foresee the time when they will learn and react without instruction – then it will be one small step to 'intelligence'.

It took Nature many millions of years to evolve the human brain. Now that same biological creation is creating an offspring. The process may take just a few decades. Then the first true robots may walk the Earth.

▲ The first electronic computer went into operation in 1943. Using bulky valves in its circuits it sprawled across 160 square metres. In the 1950s small transistors replaced valves and a modem computer like the one above takes up only a few metres. The latest computers have transistors in 'micro-chip' form reducing the size of their electronic 'brains' thousands of times. Computers are good at arithmetic, but they cannot (as yet) think for themselves.

Computer counting

1	1	110	6
10	2	111	7
11	3	1000	8
100	4	1001	9
101	5	1010	10

Computers count in binary code. The binary equivalents of decimal numbers are shown here. See if you can work out this word, coded into binary – 1010 110. Answer, page 97.

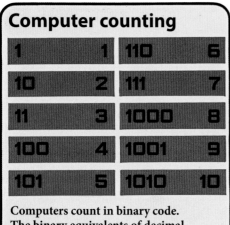

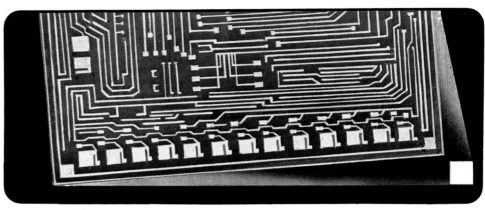

▲ Smaller and smaller is the trend in computer design. This picture, looking a bit like an aerial view of a city, is in fact an enlarged view of a micro circuit infused on a wafer-thin chip of silicon just 63 mm across. Silicon chips are already used in, for example, calculators and clocks. In the future, chip equipped machines are going to take over routine jobs from humans on a massive scale in the same way that machines took over from human muscles 200 years before.

▲ This picture shows a computer at work in the car industry. Designers have the car's shape displayed on a TV screen. The image can be viewed from any angle and changed easily until the body style is decided upon, making designing quicker and cheaper.

▲ Civilization is becoming increasingly dependent on computers. As machines take over, society becomes more vulnerable to natural or man-made disasters. If power supplies are interrupted, industries and cities, like the blacked-out town above, grind to a halt. Unless people retain basic skills and crafts, parts or all of civilization could perish. Perhaps groups of craft workers could be set up as an insurance policy against global disaster.

Man and machine – partners down the future ages

The prospect of intelligent machines should be little cause for fear. A man/machine partnership, each doing what it is best at, is more likely than that of mad robots taking over the world.

The result could be just another step along the pathway of human evolution, perhaps an entirely new breed of man, better fitted to explore the Universe.

This picture shows a possible exploration team of the future. Humans and machines work together as they study a small inhabitant of a world far away in the depths of space. In this explorer team the humans are 'in charge', though the starship's electronic brain has more capacity than the brains of all its human crew put together, and would probably override (or at least query) any orders it disagreed with.

The human-shaped machine, a true 'robot', *is* possible, but likely to be an unusual member in the ranks of the robots. Designed and built for specific functions, few robots will need exactly the same number or type of limbs as a human being.

BATTLEGROUND 2000

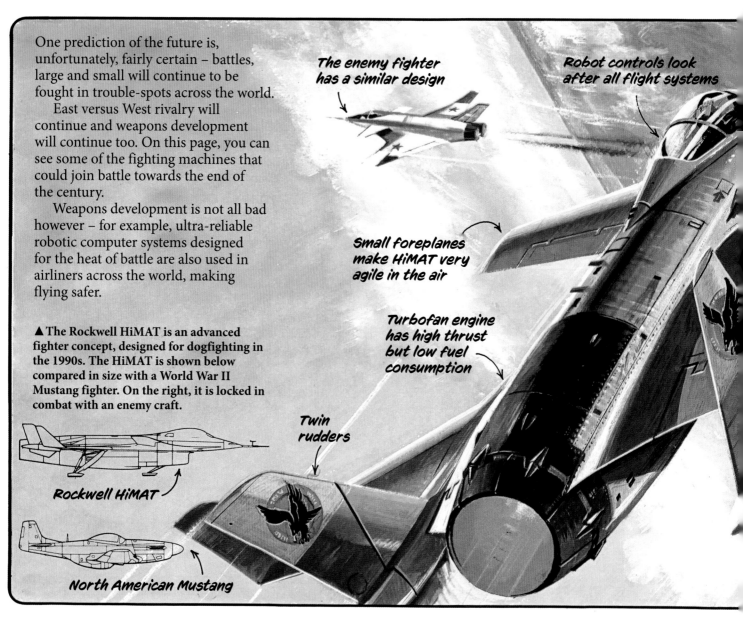

One prediction of the future is, unfortunately, fairly certain – battles, large and small will continue to be fought in trouble-spots across the world.

East versus West rivalry will continue and weapons development will continue too. On this page, you can see some of the fighting machines that could join battle towards the end of the century.

Weapons development is not all bad however – for example, ultra-reliable robotic computer systems designed for the heat of battle are also used in airliners across the world, making flying safer.

▲ The Rockwell HiMAT is an advanced fighter concept, designed for dogfighting in the 1990s. The HiMAT is shown below compared in size with a World War II Mustang fighter. On the right, it is locked in combat with an enemy craft.

The enemy fighter has a similar design

Robot controls look after all flight systems

Small foreplanes make HiMAT very agile in the air

Turbofan engine has high thrust but low fuel consumption

Twin rudders

Rockwell HiMAT

North American Mustang

1 ▲ It is night-time, as troops prepare to board a giant rocket transport. Their task to quell an uprising in a state half-way across the world. The rocket is fuelled with liquid hydrogen and liquid oxygen and is ready to go.

2 ▲ Lift-off. The troops are pressed down in their couches during the high acceleration vertical climb. In just over five minutes, the transport is nearly 100 km up and still climbing, up and out into space. The whole flight is completely robot-controlled.

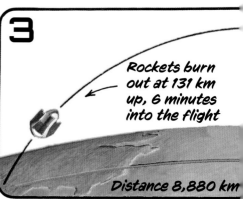

3 Rockets burn out at 131 km up, 6 minutes into the flight

Distance 8,880 km

▲ As the craft climbs, it tilts over into an arching curve to carry it toward the far side of the Earth. The outer, hydrogen-carrying tanks are dropped when their fuel is used up after six minutes of flight. The transport coas up to a maximum height of more

Single nose-mounted laser-cannon

Robot missiles are of the 'fire and forget' type. Once released, they home in on the target by themselves with no further aiming by the pilot.

▲ Although not powerful enough at present, the laser 'death ray' is eventually going to be a standard weapon. Here an armoured car carries one in place of the shell-firing cannon that it would be armed with today.

▲ Hovercraft will carry troops up the beaches in future amphibious assaults. The hovercraft above is powered by twin turbines to thrust it along at speeds up to 100 kph. Its nose drops down to form a landing ramp.

▲ 100-kph hydrofoil patrol boats already exist in small numbers. By the 1990s most, if not all, world navies will be equipped with them. The one above is firing one of several anti-shipping missiles carried in the tubes at the stern. Missiles like this make battleships and aircraft carriers easy to attack. Few navies will want these giant ships in the future. Small hydrofoils cannot stay at sea very long, so submarines will be used to refuel and re-arm them away from their shore bases.

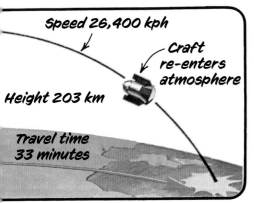

Speed 26,400 kph

Craft re-enters atmosphere

Height 203 km

Travel time 33 minutes

han 200 km, well out of the Earth's
tmosphere. It re-enters blunt tail first,
sing it as an Apollo-style heat-shield. In just
ver half an hour it will have covered nearly
,000 km at an amazing average
peed of 16,650 kph.

▲ After a period of weightlessness during the coasting part of the flight, the troops are again pressed into their couches as the craft hits the atmosphere. A shockwave curves away from the heatshield during re-entry.

▲ It is dawn as the transporter lands. Armed hovercars nose out of the cargo hold to lay a cordon round the transport before the main body of troops move off to deal with the uprising. The transporter acts as a command base for the operation.

SPEAKING TO THE STARS

Is Mankind alone in the Universe? To try and find out, astronomers have begun a search for radio signals which may have been sent by beings living on other worlds. The search began in 1960 when Dr Frank Drake used a radio telescope in the USA to listen to the stars Tau Ceti and Epsilon Eridani.

There were no tell-tale signals from other civilizations. Had there been, we may have discovered something of their science, but conversation would have been painfully slow. Radio signals would take nearly 12 years to reach us from Tau Ceti and a similar time for the replies from Earth-based transmitters to travel back.

▲ Space probes fast enough to leave the Solar System carry messages in case alien spacefarers find them millions of years in the future. Pioneers 10 and 11 (shown above) each carry an aluminium plaque showing human beings, the space craft, the planets of the Solar System and its position in the Galaxy. Two Voyager probes carry disc recordings which tell the story of life on Earth in words and sounds, from the crashing of waves and the grunts of animals to the cry of a baby.

The space-based superscope

One day a giant radio telescope like this may float above the world. Built in space by astronauts and robots, its immense antenna will receive signals from the depths of the Universe. Far more sensitive than any radio telescope on Earth, it may catch whispers from alien civilizations sent out thousands of years before.

▲ This is the radio telescope used by Dr Drake in 1960. Near Arecibo in Puerto Rico is a still larger one, over 300 metres across. In 1974 it was used to transmit a message to Messier 13, a star cluster on the edge of our galaxy.

▲ Messier 13 contains about 300,000 stars, some of which may have planets with alien creatures on them. So remote is the cluster that the message, containing information about ourselves, will take 24,000 years to get there.

Was anybody there?

What kind of creatures might receive messages from Earth? There is no way to tell, so this picture is totally fictitious. The aliens, though highly intelligent, look little like human beings. Their radio telescope is not too different though – designed for the same purpose, it has a family resemblance to those of Earth. The radio message the aliens are puzzling over tells of life on Earth. If the creatures live in the Messier 13 cluster, they are about to find out what life was like on Earth thousands of years in their past.

What happens if we contact alien beings – and they are far in advance of the human race?

Some think the result would be an exciting era of adventure and discovery. Others argue, 'Would people struggle to achieve breakthroughs in arts and science if they had the feeling that it had all been done before? A sort of racial laziness, and ultimately death, could be the result'.

Perhaps if there are aliens out there, they will not reply until they think the human race can stand the shock of contact.

What do you think – would contact be an adventure... or a disaster?

MIND OVER MATTER – THE FINAL FRONTIER?

Many people believe that, in addition to the ordinary human senses of sight, smell, taste, touch and hearing, a sixth sense lies waiting to be developed. They call it extra-sensory perception or simply ESP. It includes different abilities, such as telepathy (the ability to communicate thoughts mind to mind) and telekinesis (the ability to move objects by an act of will without touching them).

Scientists have tried to prove the reality of these and other 'strange powers' in many experiments, so far without conclusive evidence for or against. Future research should solve the problem. Could machines use ESP too? Only time will tell.

▲ When astronaut Edgar Mitchell flew to the Moon in Apollo 14, he tried to communicate telepathically with friends on Earth. His duties aboard ship sometimes interfered with his experiments but ESP-investigator Dr J.B. Rhine thought the results encouraging. Perhaps better results could be achieved if ESP could be tried on a distant planet, far from the 'telepathic interference' of the millions of other brains on Earth. Eventually mechanical ESP boosters might be built for anyone to use.

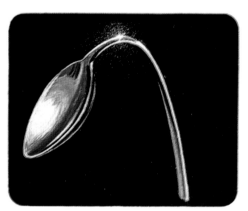

▲ Yuri Geller and others claim to bend metal objects by the power of thought. It seems like magic, but if such things can be done (and there is no proof that they can), they work because of the effect of an as yet undiscovered law of nature.

▲ There are many cases in which objects like tea cups and flower vases have suddenly – and inexplicably – taken off and smashed against walls or floors. This 'poltergeist' activity could be an example of telekinesis in action.

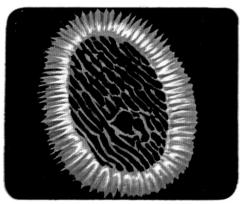

▲ Can a person heal another by the 'laying on of hands'? If so, special Kirlian photographs like this one may show the process. Streams of light surround the hand. As healing takes place, the finger tips appear to flare brightly.

Try your own telepathy experiment

Make a set of cards marked with a square, circle, cross and three wavy lines. These are the standard symbols used by professional researchers, though you can use others of your own choosing, such as the triangle shown on the right.

Choose a card at random, frame the symbol in your mind and try to 'think' it to a friend in a room next door. Russian researchers tried an experiment like this between Moscow and the science city of Novosibirsk which are 11,000 km apart. They claimed 12 of the 25 symbols were received correctly, far too many to be coincidence. See how many you get.

The ESPER battlecruiser

In the distant future people may be doing things that would seem like magic to us. Our descendants may have created bionic men and women able to boost the power of their minds to fantastic levels with mechanical robotic ESP-boosters.

In this picture, a star war is being fought with a ship crewed by ESP sensitives. Mind-power communicates with the distant Starbase. Machines and weapons are thought-controlled. The captain, hooked into the Battle Computer, has only to *think* his tactics – and they happen. Like the spoon benders of today, he may have the power to distort metal in the enemy craft and destroy their weapons. In the ship's hospital, healing hands and minds take care of battle casualties.

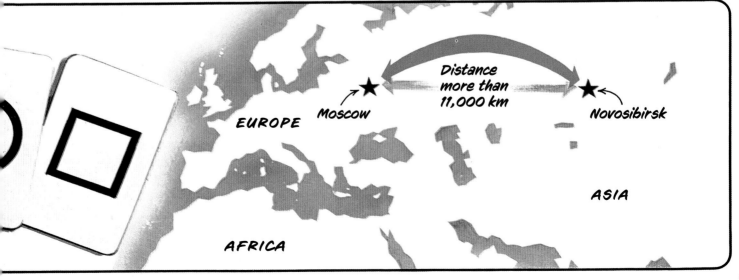

EUROPE

Moscow

Distance more than 11,000 km

Novosibirsk

AFRICA

ASIA

THE NEXT 120 YEARS: A TIMECHART

Visionaries of the late 19th and early 20th centuries like Jules Verne and H. G. Wells predicted many of the inventions which have since changed the world, including submarines, aeroplanes, spacecraft and trips to the Moon.

Even bigger changes can be expected in the next 100 years. Provided that a major atomic war can be avoided, the foreseeable future is likely to be very exciting.

Here are just some of the things which might happen, most of them within your lifetime.

1980-1990

Space telescope launched by Space Shuttle into Earth orbit . The 13 metre-long telescope enables astronomers to view stars seven times further away and 50 times fainter than possible using telescopes on Earth.

Space Shuttle demonstrates large solar-power unit as a demonstrator for the Satellite Solar Power Station.

High-energy lasers are tested in space. They are intended as weapons to disable enemy satellites.

Solar power plants set up in the Middle East to help provide cheap power for farmers.

Girder-beam building equipment tested in orbit; demonstrates ability to construct huge lightweight structures like the SSPS using automatic robots.

Wave machines developed in Britain used to produce electricity in coastal areas.

Experimental nuclear-fusion power station generates electricity successfully.

Orbital space station demonstrates that many industrial processes are cheaper and better carried out in space.

1991-2000

HiMAT-type fighters in service. Some equipped with robot pilots, flying automatically and able to fly tougher and longer missions than human pilots.

High-power lasers become standard issue on the battlefield, replacing many guns and cannon.

Reign of the robot draws near as the machine functions of vision, movement, manipulation and 'thinking' are steadily improved.

Earthquake detector flown into orbit by Space Shuttle. Used to check the unstable San Andreas fault in California, USA.

Fire-fighting machines equipped with robot command systems used in the USA to help combat forest fires.

Microcell surgery – the ability to destroy individual diseased cells in the body using laser beams – is widely practised in hospitals.

Undersea fish farms built to improve fish stocks in the oceans.

Computer systems are developed which learn from their mistakes like humans.

High-speed hovercraft troop-carrier. replace most ordinary assault craft in the world's navies.

Genetic engineering, the artificial improvement of plant or animal breeds, is used to make super-strains of wheat, corn, barley, maize and many other food crops. Better resistance to disease and bigger plants help to feed the peoples of the world.

Industrial robots increasingly take over the jobs of skilled engineers in factories.

The Replicator is developed. The device can make practically anything using material from chemicals stored nearby. The complex instructions required are masterminded by computer; laser beams place atoms and molecules into position to build any object.

Space mirrors placed in orbit to provide night-lighting on Earth. Uses of the sunlight-reflecting mirrors include city lighting and as floodlights in emergency situations like earthquake relief work.

2001-2050

First nuclear-fusion power station goes into commercial service in the USA. Obtains power from deuterium extracted from sea water.

Second-generation Space Shuttles used to carry materials into space factory orbit. Similar craft able to carry troops across the world. Boeing HLV design uses giant lake to land it back on earth.

Micro-processor mini-robot implanted in human brain. Machine helps stroke victims regain the use of their arms and legs, replacing the lost nerves.

Robots and astronauts construct first Satellite Solar Power Station in orbit. The SSPS beams a continuous beam of microwave energy to receiving stations on Earth.

Fusion power converted into microwave energy; 'exported' to other countries using a relay satellite to beam the microwaves around the world.

Men return to the Moon for the first time since 1973. This time they are surveyors, prospecting for the best site for a Moonmining colony.

Robot mining equipment landed on the Moon to extract metals from rock.

Electromagnetic catapult built on the Moon to launch raw materials to Earth-orbit space factories and to construct other habitats in space.

Robot survey craft lands on an asteroid to check its mineral worth. Giant radio-telescope placed into Earth orbit. Its task – to search for signs of other life in the Universe, intelligent life which might be broadcasting radio signals.

Asteroids used as source of mineral wealth. Small mining colonies in the Asteroid Belt are the start of an 'Outer Solar System' human civilization.

2051-2099

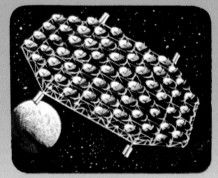

Faint signals received from space by orbiting radio-telescope. Mystery radio-waves thought to be coded message from alien creatures.

Space mirrors, under strict United Nations control, start weather-control experiments.

Computer systems effectively run the world. Only robot machine intelligence can keep track of complex problems of running a planet inhabited by 6-7,000 million people.

Practically all factory jobs taken over by industrial robots.

Scientists and super computers decode the signals from the stars received years before. First results are breakthroughs in science frontiers using the information contained in the message.

Great interest in alien message leads to the research and development of star-travelling spacecraft.

Jupiter's atmosphere mined with robot controlled balloon stations. Materials used by the human colonies now based in Earth orbit, on the Moon, Mars, and in the Asteroid Belt.

THE 22ND CENTURY AND BEYOND

Third Industrial Revolution complete: virtually all polluting industries either cleaned up or moved out into space. Man and machine gradually turn Planet Earth back into an ecologically-balanced garden planet.

Cyborgs in general use. Half-robots combining micro-electronics, power machinery and parts of human beings perform tasks impossible for humans alone.

Using computer-power and deep-space research stations, the mysteries of human ESP senses are solved. Robot ESP-boosters developed; used as brain implants for anyone who want to be an ESP-sensitive.

Artificial computer intelligence exceeds that of humans. The super robot concentrates on helping humans achieve more with the limited brain power available to them. Human adaptability makes for a man/machine partnership to explore the Universe. The birth of a new super race.

Cities in space

On these pages you can see a spaceliner leaving Astropolis, a giant space city, home for 10,000 people.

The idea of really huge, kilometres long, structures in space is quite new – an American professor called Gerald O'Neill made the first serious suggestions in 1974. Since then, various colony designs have been suggested such as the ones shown in the black and white drawings.

You can read more about building cities in space on pages 54-57.

This space city is over two kilometres long

Mirror

Sunlight

Mirrors reflect sunlight into living sphere

People live in the central sphere

Sunlight reflected off mirror lights up the city's interior

People live in this spinning tyre-like living module. Its diameter is huge, nearly two kilometres across, and it is designed to house 10,000 people

Radiators let excess heat out into space

This space city design is like the one shown in colour opposite and later on in 'Future Cities'. Like the design on the left, it is capable of housing 10,000 people in comfort

10-kilometre long transport tube

Space factory at the end of the transport tube. Powered by sunlight and solar cell system

★ *Two drawings not to the same scale*

PART TWO
FUTURE CITIES
HOME & LIVING INTO THE 21ST CENTURY

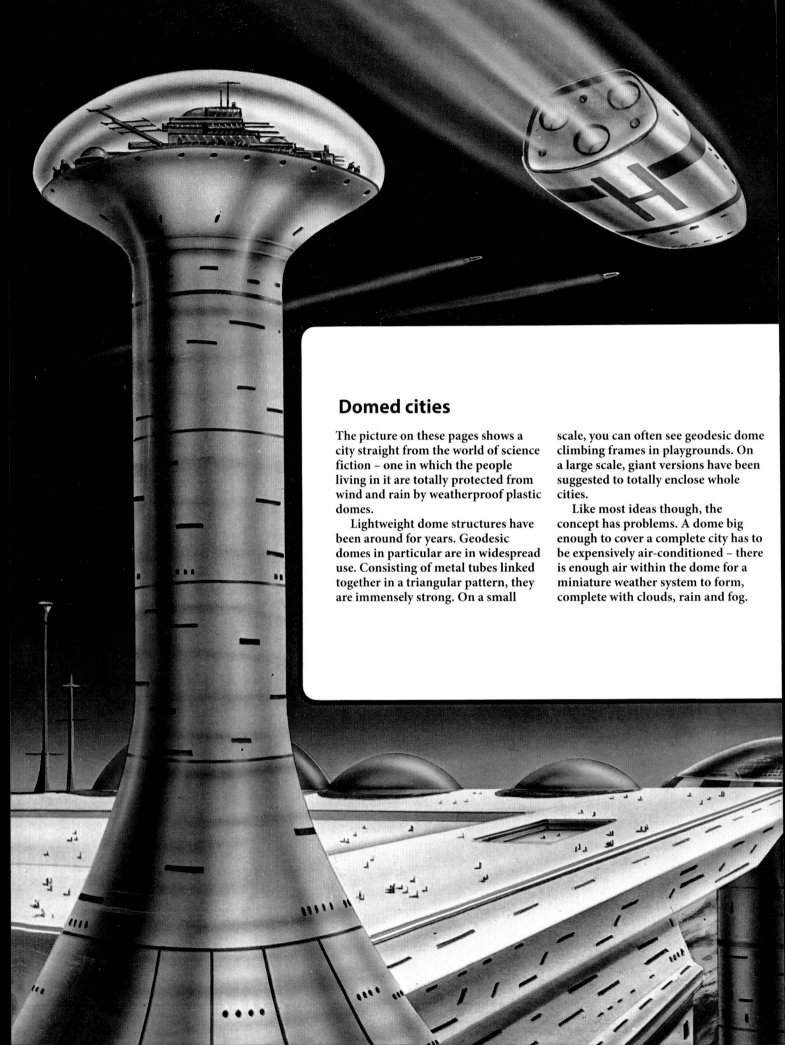

Domed cities

The picture on these pages shows a city straight from the world of science fiction – one in which the people living in it are totally protected from wind and rain by weatherproof plastic domes.

Lightweight dome structures have been around for years. Geodesic domes in particular are in widespread use. Consisting of metal tubes linked together in a triangular pattern, they are immensely strong. On a small scale, you can often see geodesic dome climbing frames in playgrounds. On a large scale, giant versions have been suggested to totally enclose whole cities.

Like most ideas though, the concept has problems. A dome big enough to cover a complete city has to be expensively air-conditioned – there is enough air within the dome for a miniature weather system to form, complete with clouds, rain and fog.

PART TWO
FUTURE CITIES
HOME & LIVING INTO THE 21st CENTURY

INTRODUCTION

In this section, you can find out about some of the amazing places to live in which might be developed in the future.

City life is not a new thing – the Greeks and Romans were building small cities thousands of years ago. What *is* a recent development is for the vast majority of a country's people to live together in cities. The problems this has brought – crime, pollution, congestion and housing problems – are common to most cities across the world.

Some people predict that these problems cannot be solved and that the large city is doomed. Others say that people like living in large groups. The evidence seems to indicate that 'super cities', consisting of many cities linked together, are developing. The super-city is not like the old industrial city, composed of solid ranks of houses and factories. It has wide swathes of parks and farmland.

The links which make a super-city are its transport systems. They enable commuters to travel hundreds of kilometres a day to and from work with little more effort than it took someone to travel a dozen kilometres in past centuries.

In the last part of this section you can see how cities could be built in other parts of the Solar System in the 21st century and beyond.

FROM CAVE DWELLINGS TO SKYSCRAPERS

On these pages you can see some of the major changes in the way people have lived over the centuries.

Today's city is a recent 'invention'. Until the Industrial Revolution of the 1700s, even the biggest city was no larger than a small modern town. With the introduction of goods producing factories, there was suddenly a necessity for many people – the workers – to live close together, near their factory.

An example of the spectacular growth of a major city is London – from the city of the Middle Ages, measuring just over two square kilometres, to today's colossus, nearly 800 times bigger.

▲ The 'city' of 350,000 years ago could have looked like this. Caves provided warmth, shelter and protection from the many fierce animals which roamed the world of our ancestors. Incredibly, cave dwellers still exist in the 20th century.

In 1971 a group of people called the Tasaday were discovered in the Philippines. Their cave entrances were high up a rock face, reached only by climbing trees or swinging from lianas like Tarzan.

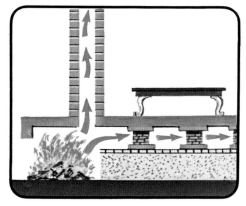

▲ The first cities were Roman. The word itself comes from the Latin *civitas,* meaning a self-governing community. The building above is a typical example of Roman architecture. It was a palace, built about 1,900 years ago. Prosperous homes had mosaic floors and underfloor heating. The city of Rome had many of the problems familiar to today's city-dwellers – overcrowding was a problem, with whole families living in one room. Fresh water and drains were only available to the rich.

▲ Underfloor central heating was a 'first' for Roman inventors. Floors were set on supports so that hot air from a furnace, kept stoked by a slave, could circulate under them. Air ducts up the walls enabled the warm air to escape.

▲ The most recent major change in cities and city life occurred as a result of the Industrial Revolution. During the 1800s, towns grew enormously as thousands of people moved from the countryside to work in the new factories which were being built. Today, most people live in large sprawling cities. This was particularly true of Europe and North America at first, but the same trends are apparent all over the world.

▲ This picture of skyscraper blocks is based on sketches made by French architect Le Corbusier in the 1920s. The idea of huge multi-storey living units surrounded by lots of parks, with wide roads for easy travel seemed a good idea

2

▲ This wintry scene is from the Northern Europe of 4,000 years ago. By this time, the Neolithic or New Stone Age, people had learned to cultivate crops and kept domestic animals for food and skins. The farmers of this period lived in houses of wood or stone. The ones pictured above are based on archaeological researches at Skara Brae off the north of Scotland where the remains of houses like them have been found. The walls were very thick and roofs had rafters made of whalebones. Animal skins kept out the weather, while a hole in the middle allowed the smoke from a fire within to escape. Life was probably quite comfortable for the Neolithic people – fireplaces, beds and cupboards, all made from stone, have been found.

4

▲ Many modern European cities developed from the castles of the Middle Ages. This one, a typical Norman design of the 10th century, was made of stone with walls up to five metres thick. The main part, the keep, was built on a small steep hill and surrounded by a strong wall. The outer, curtain, wall contained houses, workshops, stables and barns. The whole thing was designed to support itself for long periods in the event of a siege. The growth of a town around a strong central point was a natural development over the centuries. Today, few cities have their walls well preserved though the city wall of Avila in Spain is a fine example of one that still survives. The central keeps have fared better, with many throughout Europe which you can visit.

at the time. Skyscraper blocks had been built in the late 19th century, especially in the USA, but it was new materials, like concrete, steel and plate glass which made it possible to build large living blocks cheaply enough to be practicable. In theory, a tower block ought to be an ideal place to live in, but the reality has been very different. Lifts break down, flats are usually cramped. If you want to play you have to go outside – several storeys down and out of contact with your family.

It seems that city planners and architects have learnt little and that some modern cities are worse places to live in than towns of the Middle Ages. In the USA, vandalism has got so bad that blocks of flats have been demolished rather than be maintained at enormous expense. But designers are learning from mistakes made in the past and there are some hopes that future cities may be better places to live in than those of today.

Now read on... into the fantastic world of the future.

TWO TRIPS TO THE 21ST CENTURY

On these pages, you can see two sorts of city. The top one, a polluted pest-hole, already exists in at least one respect – traffic cops in the Tokyo of today have to wear smog masks. The bottom picture, a fairly clean, moderately attractive place, is possible if planners and people strive to make it so.

Some help is already to hand. People are at least aware of many of the problems of city life and are trying to solve them; and space satellites can be used for pollution control. The picture below showing northern Europe and its weather is a typical example of the clear pictures possible using 'sky-spies'.

Garden city on a cared-for planet

This scene, though not pretending to show that a perfect world is possible, nevertheless indicates that tomorrow's towns could be pleasant places to live, work and play in.

1 Electric monorail train provides an effective though not especially elegant solution to the problem of high speed travel.
2 Below the line runs a pipe network through which most bulk cargo (such as fuel, water, grain) is pumped, silently and efficiently.
3 The city is green all over, the result of a massive world-wide tree-planting scheme started in the 1980s. It is estimated by present-day researchers that every man, woman and child on Earth needs to plant a tree a day in order to keep a balance with those that are removed or killed. The world's main oxygen-producing area is, at present, the Brazilian rain-forest. This is being chopped down, slowly but surely. A balance must be kept.
4 Non-polluting jet, powered by hydrogen fuel (whose waste is water) flies quietly across the sky.
5 Fumeless electric vehicles used for local

travel. Trucks are only needed for short-distance hauls as pipe systems carry most cargo.
6 The worst excesses of mid 20th century 'brutalist' architecture are camouflaged

with flowering vines.
7 Bicycles provide the basic means of transport for people to get about over short distances. Special bikeways like this keep cyclists apart from trucks and cars.

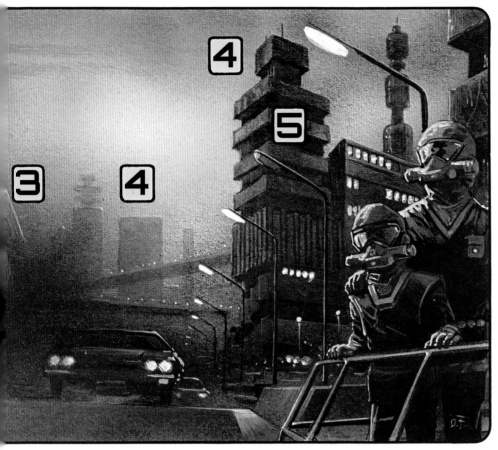

Polluted city of a dying world

If drastic steps are not taken to control pollution and to try and achieve some sort of ecological balance in the world, the picture on the left is likely to be typical of a city of the early 21st century. Its unpleasant features include:

1 Line of stunted, dying trees. At least these are still alive. In some present-day cities, planners have included plastic ones as bright, colourful, easy-clean alternatives to the real, oxygen-producing, thing.

2 Smog-laden sky. Visibility is limited and rain washes acids down from the sky. A jet trails a plume of filth.

3 Heavy trucks thunder along the pitted roadway while cars battle their way through the traffic fumes. Vehicles are running on petrol fuel, a rare but valuable item in this future world. Alternatives to petrol, such as solar or nuclear fusion power, have not been pursued, so there is nothing to replace the oil when it runs out.

4 Huge, ugly, apartment blocks are thrown up to keep pace with the rapidly increasing population of the city. Birth control measures have failed and most people are out of work and ill-fed.

5 Neglect and decay result in city systems – such as lighting – breaking down.

Power for tomorrow's towns

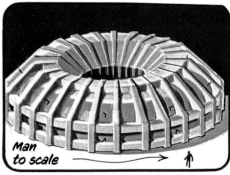

Man to scale

Present research in Europe, USA and the USSR indicates that the 'Tokamak' nuclear fusion reactor could provide much of the energy for the people of tomorrow's towns. A Tokamak generates an intense magnetic field in its doughnut-shaped reaction chamber to burn atoms of deuterium and tritium fuel. The result, like a controlled H-bomb, is heat and light. The heat can be used to generate electricity. Deuterium, which comes from seawater, is virtually limitless in supply. Tritium supplies will take 50,000 years to run out. One litre of the fuel is equivalent, in terms of energy, to about 300 litres of oil.

A HOUSE OF THE FUTURE

The features of this house, based on studies by the American space agency NASA, could well be found on most new houses built in the future.

The style of the house is only one architect's idea – around the world the basic 'look' would change according to local tastes.

Size too, would vary according to the amount of money available. The house shown is a large one with a separate garage for an electric car, but even a one-bedroom house could share many of the energy saving design features.

Solar heating

Sun's rays

Cold water

Black panel

Glass panel

Warmed water

Solar panels on the roof help heat water for the house, saving energy. The panels take the chill off the mains water before an ordinary immersion heater boosts it to hot-bath temperatures.

Insulation

Wood boarding

Polystyrene

Glass fibre

Bricks

Out side

Inside

Latest studies indicate that really good insulation (just one type is shown above) can save huge quantities of energy. Energy savings mean that oil is saved, putting off the day when supplies run out.

Self-sufficiency

Many countries have to import vast amounts of food. Tomorrow's towns could have lots of areas for people to grow food on. A house like this one, with its own garden, has lots of vegetable growing space. New seed varieties should ensure that even amateur gardeners get a good crop.

TV, radio and telephone reception will increasingly be via space satellites. Dish aerials like this could well be a common sight on rooftops of the 1990s.

Crime prevention should be a major concern for the 1980s and '90s. This lock is computerised – it scans and recognises the fingerprints of members of the family who have been 'keyed' into the computer's memory bank.

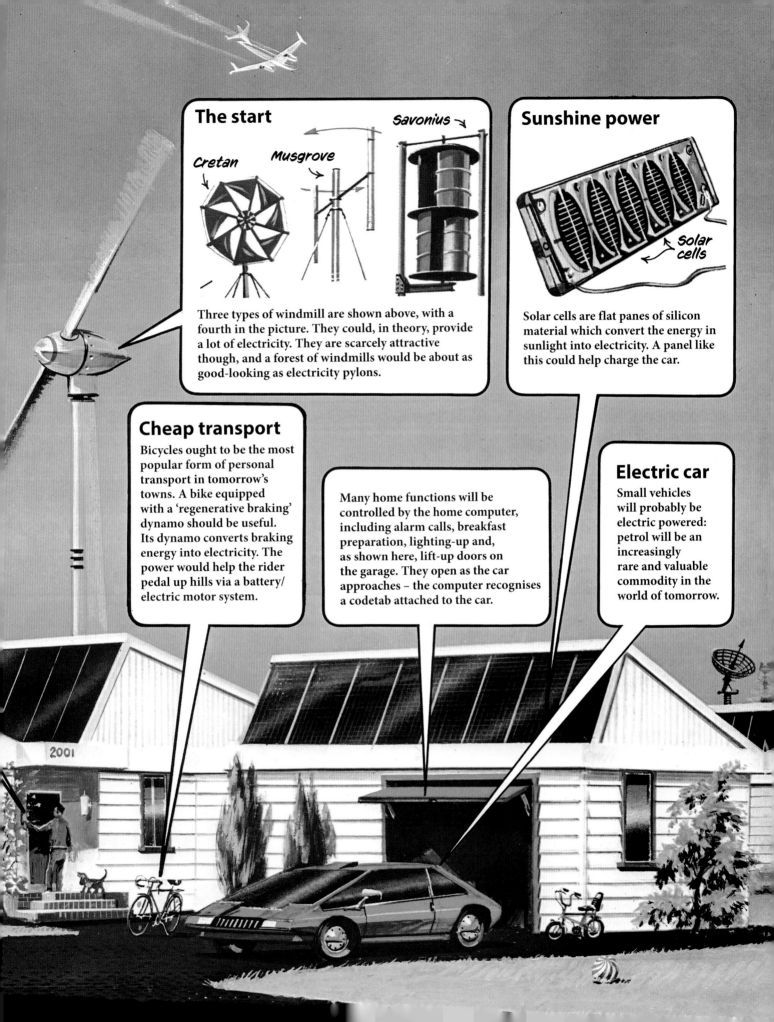

The start

Cretan

Musgrove

Savonius

Three types of windmill are shown above, with a fourth in the picture. They could, in theory, provide a lot of electricity. They are scarcely attractive though, and a forest of windmills would be about as good-looking as electricity pylons.

Sunshine power

Solar cells

Solar cells are flat panes of silicon material which convert the energy in sunlight into electricity. A panel like this could help charge the car.

Cheap transport

Bicycles ought to be the most popular form of personal transport in tomorrow's towns. A bike equipped with a 'regenerative braking' dynamo should be useful. Its dynamo converts braking energy into electricity. The power would help the rider pedal up hills via a battery/electric motor system.

Many home functions will be controlled by the home computer, including alarm calls, breakfast preparation, lighting-up and, as shown here, lift-up doors on the garage. They open as the car approaches – the computer recognises a codetab attached to the car.

Electric car

Small vehicles will probably be electric powered: petrol will be an increasingly rare and valuable commodity in the world of tomorrow.

2001

COMPUTERS IN THE HOME

The picture on the right takes you into the living room of a house of the future. The basics will probably be similar – windows, furniture, carpet and TV. There will be one big change though – the number of electronic gadgets in use.

The same computer revolution which has resulted in calculators and digital watches could, through the 1980s and '90s, revolutionise people's living habits.

Television is changing from a box to stare at into a useful two-way tool. Electronic newspapers are already available – pushing the button on a handset lets you read 'pages' of news, weather, puzzles and quizzes.

TV-telephones should be a practical reality by the mid 1980s. Xerox copying over the telephone already exists. Combining the two could result in millions of office workers being able to work at home if they wish. There is little need to work in a central office if a computer can store records, copiers can send information from place to place and people can talk on TV-telephones.

Many people may prefer to carry on working in an office with others, but for those who are happy at home, the savings in travelling time would be useful. Even better would be the money saved on transport costs to and from work.

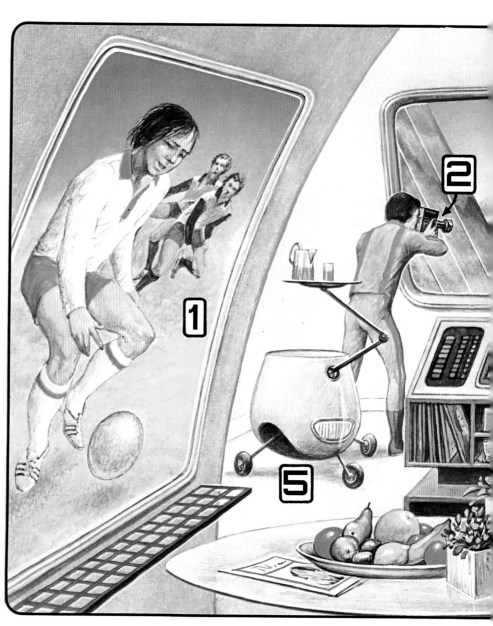

▲ The magic of laser-holography, a new technique which creates 3-D pictures apparently out of thin air, could result in business conferences like the one shown above. On the left the heads of a branch office have just come in to their boardroom, first thing in the morning. Across the table is their boss. He is in the head office of the company in the centre of a major city thousands of miles away. It is night-time there and is the end of his day. 3-D cameras hanging from the ceilings of each room create the illusion of a compete room with the two sides present (this picture has been split down the middle to avoid confusion). Electronic conferences like this would save enormous amounts of time, money and energy.

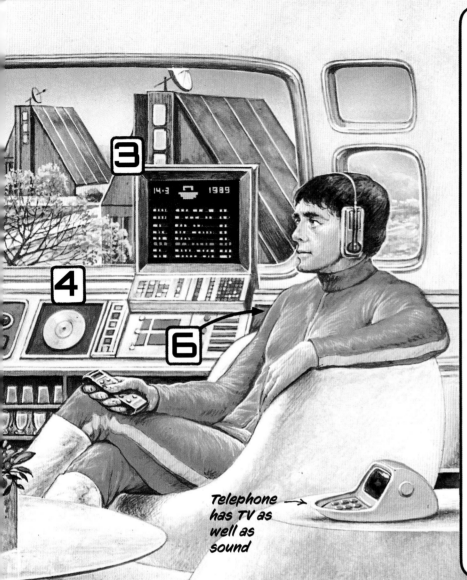

The electronic household

This living room has many electronic gadgets which are either in use already or are being developed for people to buy in the 1980s.

1 Giant-size TV. Based on the designs already available, this one has a super-bright screen for daylight viewing and stereo sound system.

2 Electronic video movie camera, requires no film, just a spool of tape. Within ten years video cameras like this could be replaced by 3-D holographic recorders.

3 Flat screen TV. No longer a bulky box, TV has shrunk to a thickness of less than five centimetres. This one is used to order shopping via a computerised shopping centre a few kilometres away. The system takes orders and indicates if any items are not in stock.

4 Video disc player used for recording off the TV and for replaying favourite films.

5 Domestic robot rolls in with drinks. One robot, the Quasar, is already on sale in the USA. Reports indicate that it may be little more than a toy however, so it will be a few years before 'Star Wars' robots tramp through our homes.

6 Mail slot. By 1990, most mail will be sent in electronic form. Posting a letter will consist of placing it in front of a copier in your home or at the post office. The electronic read-out will be flashed up to a satellite, to be beamed to its destination. Like many other electronic ideas, the savings in time and energy could be enormous.

Telephone has TV as well as sound →

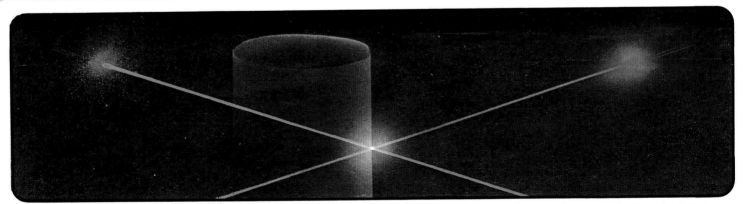

▲ Today it is possible to copy a photograph or document in a Xerox copier. In the future, it should be as simple to copy a three-dimensional object. Such a 3-D copier already exists in prototype form. It works like this: a transparent tank is filled with special liquid which solidifies in the presence of light of a particular colour, just as photographic paper darkens when exposed to light. Two different coloured laser beams criss-cross the tank. Where they cross, their light mixes and changes colour. At that point the liquid solidifies. By following pre-set instructions the lasers can 'carve-out' any shape in the tank. By varying the lasers' colour and by varying the ingredients of the liquid, it may be possible to create virtually anything.

THE ELECTRONIC REVOLUTION

City dwellers of tomorrow could have a small gadget of enormous benefit – a wristwatch radio-telephone. With a wristwatch radio, you could talk to anyone, wherever you happened to be.

The secret of the system lies in the super-powerful satellite shown on the page opposite. Present-day satellites are fairly simple, just repeaters, with expensive ground stations. A future satellite designed for wrist-radios (which might be nicknamed 'ristos') would be the expensive part of the system. A risto would sell for about the same price as a pocket calculator and weigh no more than a few grammes.

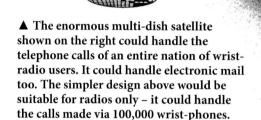

▲ The enormous multi-dish satellite shown on the right could handle the telephone calls of an entire nation of wrist-radio users. It could handle electronic mail too. The simpler design above would be suitable for radios only – it could handle the calls made via 100,000 wrist-phones.

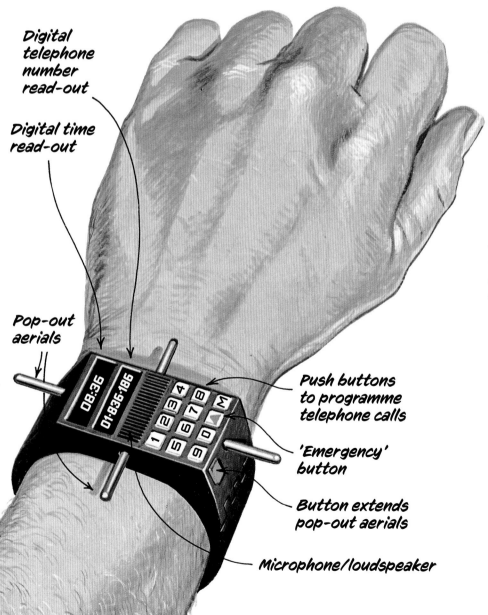

Digital telephone number read-out

Digital time read-out

Pop-out aerials

Push buttons to programme telephone calls

'Emergency' button

Button extends pop-out aerials

Microphone/loudspeaker

▲ Instant voting could be a feature of a risto-using city. Important questions could be asked either over the risto or using TV as shown here. Using computers to count the votes, 100 million votes could be counted in an hour.

▲ Probably the best reason for having a risto would be for use in a life-or-death situation. This future scene shows a boat going down in a storm at sea. The lone survivor presses her panic button before passing into unconsciousness.

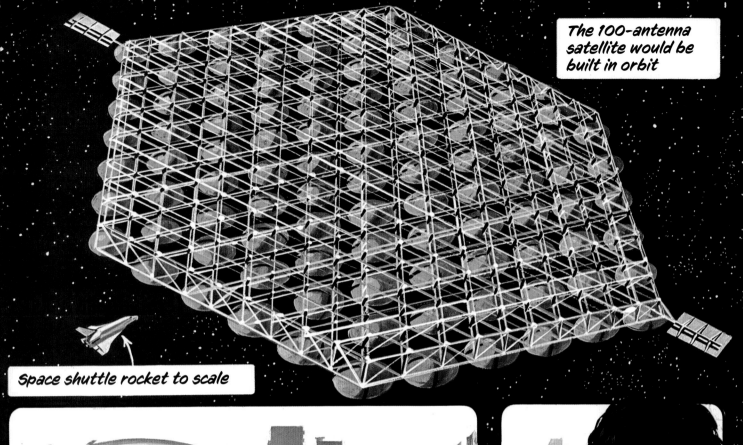

Space shuttle rocket to scale

▲ Crime in cities could get a knock from the risto. Police would all be equipped with ristos, making equipment in patrol cars unnecessary. Conversations would be 'scrambled' so they could not be overheard and in an emergency, police ristos would have priority over others. In the picture above two thieves have just stolen a car – its owner presses the emergency button on his risto to get help quickly. Emergency calls could be free, though computers would add up the price of other ones.

▲ If you were late for an appointment, it would be easy to let the other people know. The risto doubles as a watch too, continuously corrected by a time pulse from the satellite overhead. There would be few excuses for being late!

A continuous search-and-rescue signal comes from the waterproof risto. Helicopters, based on the floating sea-city, can home-in on the signal. If they are in time, the survivor will be having a hot drink in a few minutes.

▲ It ought to be impossible to get lost in tomorrow's world, in a city or out of it. This city dweller is on holiday at the seaside. The Sun is going down and the sand dunes seem endless. By punching out an enquiry number on his risto, he can ask for guidance back to the nearest town. In an emergency – perhaps the tide is coming up – a 'panic' button would bring help.

45

SEA CITY 2000

This pyramid-shaped structure is a self-contained floating city, an idea that has been suggested as an alternative to building more suburbs or tower blocks.

American architect Buckminster Fuller suggested the concept of floating cities in the 1960s. The design shown here uses some of his ideas, together with those of another architect, Paolo Soleri, to produce an archology – a blending of architecture and ecology to solve some of the problems of city life.

An archology is basically one huge building, with shops, schools, playgrounds and homes all within walking distance of each other. There would be no need for cars, so there would be no congestion. All city wastes would be recycled, the archology being designed to keep in ecological balance with its environment.

Dish-shaped antenna beams microwave energy, generated by the solar cells, to a receiver on the nearby coast. There it will be converted into electricity

Dome-covered machinery to convert raw materials into finished products

Lightweight cargo plane coming in for a landing

Craft like this high-speed hydrofoil keep the sea-city in touch with land cities and other archologies on the oceans

Underwater equipment designed to support mineral mining and fish farming, which are the two main activity of this sea city, floating off the African coast

The sides of the pyramid are covered with electricity-producing solar cells

The outer surfaces of the front and back of the pyramid are balconies for the living apartments just inside

Inside the pyramid are schools, shops, play areas and meeting halls

◄ A floating city like this could be a good place for its people to work in. Jobs include mining the local sea bed for minerals – sure to be an important activity in the 21st century. Fish farming would be important too, the city being equipped with its own freezing and packing plants. For sea cities based in warm areas like the Mediterranean, tourism could be important, with holidaymakers making underwater excursions in submarines. It might be possible for small sea cities to be mobile, drifting on ocean currents as they follow valuable seabed mineral deposits.

▲ This picture shows Buckminster Fuller's idea for a floating community. A city like this was designed to contain the shops, schools and homes for 5,000 people. At the base is a harbour and yacht marina.

▲ Heavy-lift airships like this one, based on a NASA study, could be used to transport goods between a sea city and land. The cities would be fairly close to shore, especially if it proved practicable to 'export' electricity by microwave.

THE TALLEST SKYSCRAPER EVER

This fantastic 'beanstalk' is a city built for the stars. It is literally a lift shaft up to Earth orbit.

The building would avoid the noise and atmospheric pollution caused by rockets taking off and landing as the bullet-shaped 'rockets' whizz up and down in sealed tubes.

The idea of a structure like this is not a new one – it originated with a Russian, Yuri Artsutanov. The well-known writer, Arthur C. Clarke, has written a book dramatising the construction of such a tower.

As you can see from the small pictures on the left, building the beanstalk would be extremely complex and certainly not possible in the immediate future. But if it is ever constructed, people and payloads could travel up to orbit as easily as they can travel across today's world in a jet airliner.

5 A city for the stars

The base of the beanstalk would be a thriving community of several thousand people – a cross between a small town and a large airport of today.

The beanstalk is set amid tropical forest – it is exactly on the Earth's equator. Visitors and passengers for the shuttles arrive in high speed electric tube trains, running above the forest to avoid chopping trees down. Once inside, people would find booking facilities together with shops, restaurants and hotels.

To take a lift into space a passenger first goes below ground – the shuttles start their journey hundreds of metres down, fired upwards like peas from a shooter. The glowing tubes contain no air, so there would be little friction to slow the progress of the shuttles. Electro-magnetic motors boost the shuttles' speeds high enough to climb up to orbit.

▲ Construction of the beanstalk starts with a satellite placed in orbit 36,000 km above the Earth's equator. In this synchronous orbit, the satellite stays over the same point on the Earth.

▲ A cable is slowly extended towards the Earth. At the same time one the same length is extended the other way to balance it. The length of the two cables will eventually total an amazing 72,000 km.

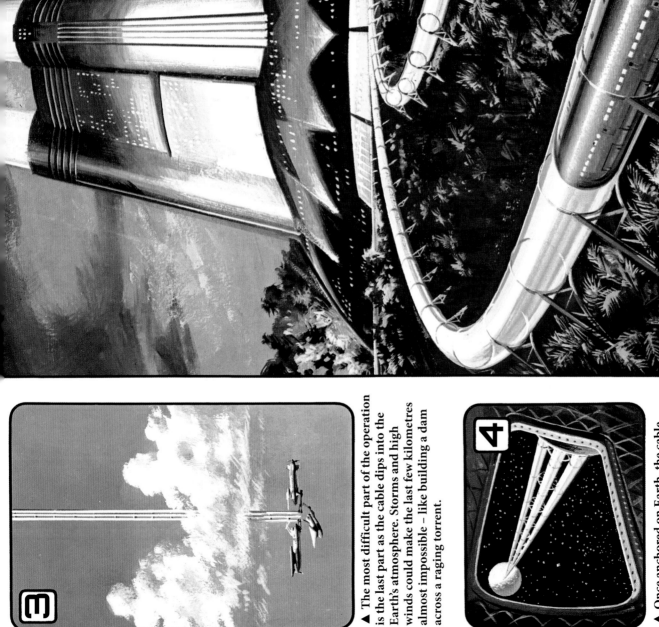

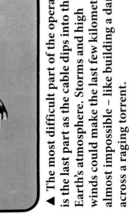

▲ The most difficult part of the operation is the last part as the cable dips into the Earth's atmosphere. Storms and high winds could make the last few kilometres almost impossible – like building a dam across a raging torrent.

▲ Once anchored on Earth, the cable could be thickened and added to so that it could eventually be a lift-shaft for shuttle craft. This view shows an astronaut's-eye-view through a porthole of the satellite.

MOON BASE

Less fantastic than a beanstalk is the idea of a Moonbase. When the first man landed on the Moon in 1969, many people expected there would be a permanent manned station very soon afterward. In fact, there has been no one on the Moon since the last Apollo trip in 1972.

The USA no longer has any Apollo moonships and there are no plans to send any craft using the Space Shuttle to launch them. So until the 1990s at least, there are not going to be any astronauts on the Moon. Perhaps the Russians have secret plans to send cosmonauts....

In any event a Moonbase like the one shown here is very unlikely to exist much before 2000. Its purpose would be partly for scientific research and partly for the practical purpose of starting mining operations.

Armstrong, the first city on the Moon

This base is named after Neil Armstrong, the first man to walk on the Moon, in 1969. It is a 'second phase' base. The 'first phase' base would probably re-use rocket fuel tanks as the basis for its living quarters. This one is more permanent, and most important, is being used for the practical purpose of moonmining.

1 Moonshuttle coming in to land from Earth orbit.

2 The Earth, low in the sky. The base is situated near the Moon's south pole near the Leibnitz Mountains.

3 Mining area. Useful minerals include oxygen, titanium and aluminium.

4 Landing pad for shuttles.

5 Moonjeep, ready to meet the visitors aboard the ship from Earth.

6 Most of the base is underground like Antarctic bases on Earth. This multi-storey dome houses the computer and command equipment. The 'Moonies' can live in shirtsleeve comfort in their snug underground 'town'.

7 Domes are made of compressed Moonsoil, a kind of lunar concrete.

8 Communications equipment. Apart from radio and TV, messages could be sent using laser beams.

9 Airtight underground tunnels connect the various domes. The longer ones have moving pavements built-in to speed the travel of the Moon dwellers.

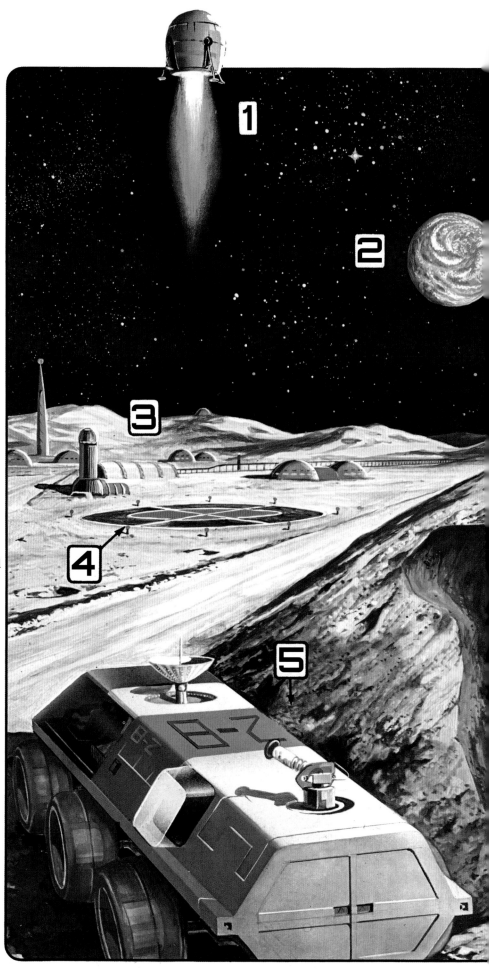

Mining – on the Moon?

It may seem a difficult place to go in order to carry out mining operations, but some vital resources are already running short here on Earth. At the moment, it is difficult to say exactly what will (or will not) be available or be worth mining on the Moon. It is worth remembering that the 15th century voyages to the New World, now the USA, were made without knowing much about the country. Living conditions on the Moon may seem severe, but Earthbound miners have opened up some very difficult areas – from the stormy North Sea to frozen Alaska.

▲ These sketches, by R. A. Smith, were made in the 1950s, yet they remain as accurate renderings of how a Moonbase might look. This picture shows a dome being constructed, rather like an igloo. Instead of ice, it is made of Moonrock.

▲ A good transport system might be an electric monorail like this one, soaring high over cracks, craters and fissures. The first monorail route would be between the domes of the base and nearby mine workings.

▲ Air purification plant for a Moonbase. The first Moon travellers took their own air with them. It ought to be possible for machinery like this to extract oxygen from Moonsoil and rocks.

THE OLYMPIC GAMES, YEAR 2020

If Armstrong, or a base like it, is a success, then after 20 years or so it ought to be much bigger – a true Moon city. Whole families could be living on the Moon. The children would regard it as home and perhaps puzzle over the pictures of Earth's green fields their homesick parents hang on the walls of their living module.

The 'Moonies' (as they might be called) might want the prestige of holding a major world event. The best thing might well be the First Interplanetary Olympics. On these pages you can read the story of the Games of 2020 as they just might happen....

▲ It is 11.00 a.m. at Earthport, Africa's main spacebase. A few minutes before, an athlete, Yuri Umtali, completed his journey from Athens in Greece, carrying the Olympic Flame. All is ready as he boards the shuttle-craft waiting for him on the launch pad: the torch is placed in a special clamp and Yuri is strapped into his acceleration couch by a stewardess. As the countdown reaches zero, the shuttle's motors fire, and, slowly at first, the ship lifts off the launch pad.

▲ Less than 30 minutes later the shuttle is approaching a giant wheel-shaped space station circling the Earth. For the shuttle, the journey is over as it noses gently into the station's main spacelock. For Yuri, the journey has barely begun.

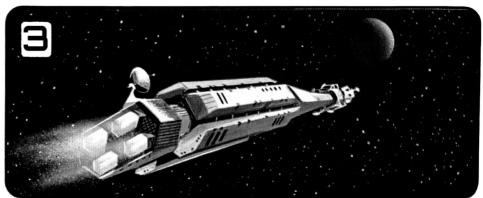

▲ The next stage is the long three-day journey from Earth orbit to Lunar orbit. The craft is a comfy spaceliner on which (reporters and video cameras permitting) Yuri can relax. The craft to be used for the actual landing at Armstrong is a replica of the 'Eagle' module, the first craft to land on the Moon over half a century before. The craft looks the same, but its 'primitive' power, guidance and life-support systems have been replaced by newer robot-controlled ones.

▲ The Moon landing was uneventful and here Yuri pauses for the video-recorders as he jogs towards the newly-built stadium. The Flame is in a special globular container. In its handle is an oxygen cylinder, in its top is a fan to provide a draught. Without this, the flame would go out – there is no air on the Moon. Hidden from view behind Yuri is a newly erected statue of a spacesuited golfer – the first 'sportsman' on the Moon, Alan Shepard Jr, who practised drives when he went to the Moon in 1971. In a few minutes, the Olympic Games of the year 2020 will start. The stadium is covered with a huge plexiglass dome – the visitors from Earth will have a fine view of their home world through it.

The Lunar high jump – 14 metres up

Yuri Umtali has lit the sacred flame and the Games have started.

One of the most extraordinary things about the Lunar Olympics is the effect the Moon's low gravity – one sixth that of the Earth – has on the sports. A grown man only weighs about 11 kilogrammes there and it ought to be possible to jump up to 14 metres high. As this picture shows, special equipment is needed to replace the bar.

The thousands of Moonies in the crowd will feel proud of the new records being set, even though they know that many of them will have to be handicapped to make a fair comparison with existing Earth records.

It is unlikely that native Moonies will set any interplanetary records, as their muscles, used to the tiny pull of the Moon's gravity, will be no match for the tough muscles of the Earth athletes. Perhaps a handicapping system will be devised to take that into account too.

CITIES IN THE SKY/1

The visitors of the 2020 Olympics might be from the Moon, the Earth, and – from giant cities hanging in space near the two worlds.

The idea of cities in space providing living space for thousands of people sounds utterly fantastic, yet in 1974 a professor at Princeton University in the USA, Gerard O'Neill, came up with suggestions for such structures. Since then, the idea of space as the 'High Frontier' has caught the imagination of many people across the world.

If building cities in space does prove possible, the conquest of space may present a challenge for people on an overcrowded Earth.

▲ Living in space is not a new idea. This sketch from the 1920s illustrates Russian scientist Konstantin Tsiolkovski's concept for a rotating spaceship in which green plants could be grown to provide a constant supply of fresh oxygen for the crew.

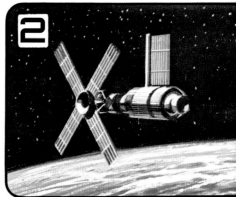

▲ The first successful space station was called Skylab. It was a fuel tank fitted out with many of the comforts of home. Three groups of American astronauts stayed in the craft in 1973 and 1974 for up to three months at a time. The

▲ To build really big space-stations, true 'space cities', it is necessary to have a cheap source of materials. The Moon could be the best place to find them, as few Earth politicians would wish to see their country's resources being rocketed off into space. The Moon is untouched territory, and its soil is rich in such materials as oxygen, calcium and aluminium. In the picture above, bulldozers are shown shifting soil in a surface mine near a Moonbase. The soil will be shaped into metre-square cubes by machinery nearby. Another advantage of using the Moon as a source of supply is that it has very low gravity, just one sixth that of Earth, so it is easier to get the material off into space.

▲ The moonsoil-cubes are blasted off the Moon, not by rocket power, but by an electro-magnetic catapult. Powered by solar cells, the catapult could send a cube every few minutes into a very precise trajectory that would take it to the point selected for the construction of the space city. In this picture, a soil cube is passing through a 'gate' which automatically checks speed and aim.

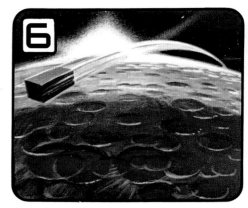

▲ The cube's destination is called L5. It is a point in space at which the gravity fields of Earth and Moon cancel each other out. This makes it a stable point at which to construct a giant space city.

Russians have also been busy with their Salyut space stations. They have carried out experiments in space welding and making electronic components. It may be possible to make some electronic components very cheaply in orbit.

▲ The Space Shuttle is the USA's first reusable spacecraft. On its way up into space, it will normally cast off its huge fuel tank when empty. It would be easy to 'do a Skylab' with the tank though, and take it up into orbit as the basis for a space station.

Even one tank would give plenty of room – it measures 46.8 metres long by 8.4 metres wide. By the late 1980s, 'tank-stations' like the one above could be a regular feature in space, with Shuttles visiting with supplies every few weeks.

▲ Various types of space city have been proposed. This one, shown under construction at L5, is based on a scheme suggested in 1975. If building a huge – over two kilometres long – structure like this proves practicable, it will provide a comfortable place for 10,000 people to live in. The two small spheres in the picture are 'construction shacks', pressurised and airconditioned modules in which to make parts for the city. Lunar soil cubes collected nearby are used for raw materials. Construction of the space city would take several years, but once the outer shell is complete the inside can be filled with air. Fitting-out can then be started. Perhaps the first space habitat would be called Astropolis – star city.

CITIES IN THE SKY/2

Once the structure of Astropolis is complete, the space city has to be made fit to live in.

Obvious essentials are air and water. The other essential, if the space-colonists are to lead anything like a normal life, is gravity.

If astronauts live for long periods in zero-gravity, their muscles waste away and their bones get brittle. Special exercises can reduce these effects, but the aim of Astropolis is to give settlers an Earthlike environment.

Scientists cannot make artificial gravity, but a similar effect can be gained by spinning Astropolis on its axis. The resulting centrifugal force plants the feet of colonists firmly on the inner surface of the city's main living sphere, resulting in a weird 'inside-out' world.

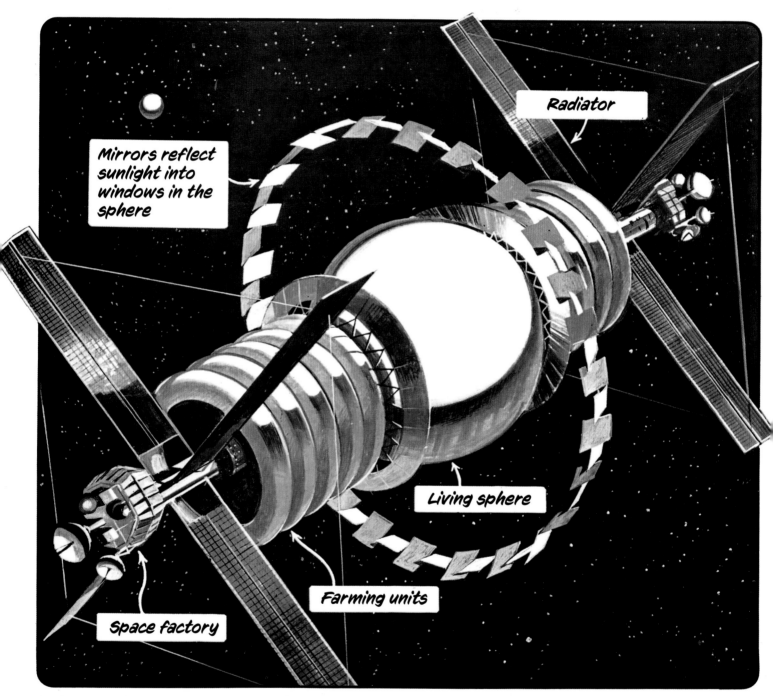

Radiator

Mirrors reflect sunlight into windows in the sphere

Living sphere

Farming units

Space factory

▲ This picture shows the city of Astropolis as it might appear from a few kilometres away. At its bottom left is a space factory, making solar energy units to provide electricity for people on Earth. The two big crosses are radiators to get rid of waste heat from the factory and Astropolis's life-support systems. The doughnut rings are 'farms', providing fresh food. The central sphere is the main living area, providing room for 10,000 people. Astropolis would start off with only 2000 or so, but the colonists would marry and have space-children, so they would need lots of spare room. As space cities go, Astropolis is by no means large – the central sphere is about 500 metres across. A walk around the equator would take about 20 minutes.

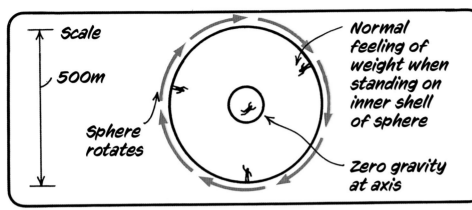

▲ This is a cross-section through the spinning central sphere of Astropolis. To a colonist 'down' is 'out'. You can get a similar centrifugal 'gravity' effect by whirling a bucket of water round and over your head.

You will see (if you are careful!) that the water stays in the bucket, even when it is whizzing over your head.

Near the axis of Astropolis, however, the gravity effect is less, and at the axis there is no gravity at all.

▲ A place like this would probably be popular with the colonists. It is a zero-gravity play-room, placed in a compartment in the axis of Astropolis. People can zoom about as perfumed air-currents play over them.

▲ A little further away from the axis, a low-gravity swimming pool like this would be possible. Divers can climb up the stairs at the end, float into the central axis, then launch themselves in lazy somersaults before they splash into the water.

▲ Out at 'ground' level, colonists look at the far end of the sphere, the central axis coming out over their heads. The colonists weigh the same as they would on Earth. The blue 'river' is a tinted window; the view, out into the depths of space.

The tropical appearance of Astropolis was decided by the city planners. Other space cities could have almost any climate or appearance, depending only on the wishes of the people living there.

▲ The 'doughnut-rings' are the city's farms. This cross-section of two rings shows how they might look. The top floor is used for vegetables and other crops, the lower two for livestock such as chickens, goats and rabbits.

▲ This space farmer needs an oxygen mask to work in one of the greenhouses. The air is specially enriched with carbon dioxide, poisonous to human beings, but providing a big boost to the growth of vegetables.

▲ Houses in Astropolis might not be too different from those on Earth. A space farmer returning after a hard day's work could come home, switch on the video-news, have a bath and supper. Later on, a visit to the theatre should be possible.

COLONIZING OTHER WORLDS

Building cities on the Moon and in space could be successful, but people may still prefer the wind, rain and open skies of Earth.

On the Moon there is little alternative to domes and tunnels. Astropolis, for all its natural landscaping, is small and confined. The other planets of the Solar System are too hot, too cold or have poisonous atmospheres.

So is there any alternative to the domed cities of science fiction on other worlds? At least one, according to American scientist Carl Sagan. His idea is to create a new Eden, from what is at the present the hell-world of Venus.

▲ Venus, named after the Roman goddess of love was misnamed. It is covered in choking clouds of sulphuric acid and its atmosphere is poison carbon dioxide. The surface of Venus roasts at a spectacular 480°C   twice as hot as a kitchen oven.

▲ If there is life on Venus, Sagan's plan ought to be dismissed immediately. Man has a poor reputation for protecting other species on Earth, let alone wiping them out on other worlds. If Venus is lifeless however, a fleet of spacecraft would set off.

5 The 'Big Rain'

Here you can see Ark II picking up speed. As oxygen replaces carbon dioxide, the atmosphere of Venus starts to clear a little. Heat, presently trapped, will escape into space and the temperature will start to drop.

Eventually water vapour will collect and the first rain will fall. It will not get as far as the surface, boiling to steam before it gets there. But each time it rains, surface temperatures drop a little. Eventually, a scene like the one shown should be possible. Here, the first manned vehicles are setting out on an exploration of the surface, formerly available only to toughly-built robots. Surrounding the explorers is the thundering torrent of the 'Big Rain' – the excess water vapour of an entire atmosphere smashing down.

There is only enough water vapour to result in a 30 cm deep covering on the surface, and one idea to provide more is to 'bomb' the planet. Comets, which often contain water in the form of ice, could be redirected toward Venus by the blast of nuclear explosions. They would melt as they entered Venus' atmosphere, spraying water vapour into it. A giant dust cloud could be orbited between Venus and the Sun to help cool the planet down. Eventually, people might be able to live on a newly-habitable world.

It is important to realise that these are ideas only; it may be centuries before the advanced technology required to perform feats of 'planetary engineering' is developed.

▲ Once in orbit around Venus, automatic controls aboard the ships start firing off tiny torpedoes into the atmosphere below. Inside each torpedo is a colony of tough bacteria, ready to 'eat' the atmosphere of Venus.

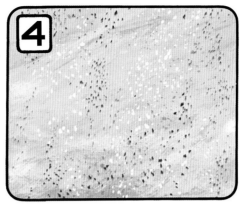

▲ The hardy bacteria – a form of algae – consume the carbon dioxide atmosphere, releasing the oxygen content of it as waste. The algae will feed – and reproduce – slowly converting the poison gases to what is, to us, vital oxygen.

Genetic engineering

Suppose the 'Venus Plan' fails or is only partly successful? Future medical science may make it possible to create new varieties of human being so they can live in places where the rest of us cannot.

Genetic engineering – modifying the structure of organisms – is already possible in agriculture: plant types are continually being improved to give better yields, bigger fruit and stronger resistance to disease. In the future, humans may be modified. The results could be higher intelligence, better physique and, like crops, stronger resistance to disease.

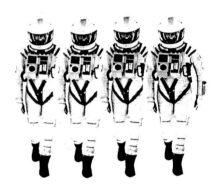

Making identical creatures, a process called cloning, is also a possibility. Clones can already be made of frogs; in a few years it should be possible to clone domestic animals such as prize cattle. After that, the frightful vision of hordes of identical people – perhaps an army of super-soldiers – could become a terrifying reality.

▲ In the end, attempts to change other worlds may be a total failure. If so, then colonists on other worlds will probably live in cities like the one above, protected from the elements by huge plastic domes.

EMPIRE OF THE SUN

By the end of the 21st century people could be living in cities on Earth, the Moon, in space and on Venus. What then? Assuming that a nuclear war does not knock civilization back to the Stone Age, experts think that Man could eventually colonize the entire Solar System. A major step would be to use the Asteroid Belt, thousands of rocks orbiting between Mars and Jupiter, as a source of raw materials. Eventually, the Belt itself could be colonized, with cities being made from hollowed-out asteroids.

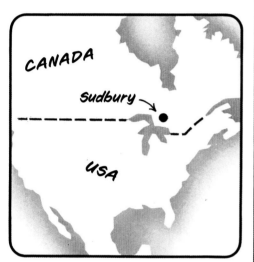

▲ Millions of years ago a gigantic meteorite fell in what is now Sudbury, in Canada. Half the world's supply of nickel comes from it. 'We were mining an asteroid and few people realised it,' says Professor O'Leary, Head of the Physics Department at Princeton University.

▲ The moons of Mars are thought to be asteroids, captured by Mars' gravitational pull. In the future the moons, named Phobos and Deimos, could be used to provide raw material to build colonies in orbit around Mars.

Asteroid City

By the late 21st century, the Asteroid Belt will probably be the new frontier for miners and explorers. Space cities like the one shown above would float in space. Smelting plants would process materials while space freighters take the refined metals to Earth orbit for use in space factories. Others would supply communities on and around Mars.

Asteroid City could well be the future version of a small cowtown of the old Wild West. Miners, returning from months out in the 'belt' would use the city for rest and relaxation. Gunfights maybe – though with laser-pistols rather than Colt .45s. Other features of the city include:
1 Small asteroid being received through the main spacelock of the city's smelting plant. It will be melted down and processed for its metal content.

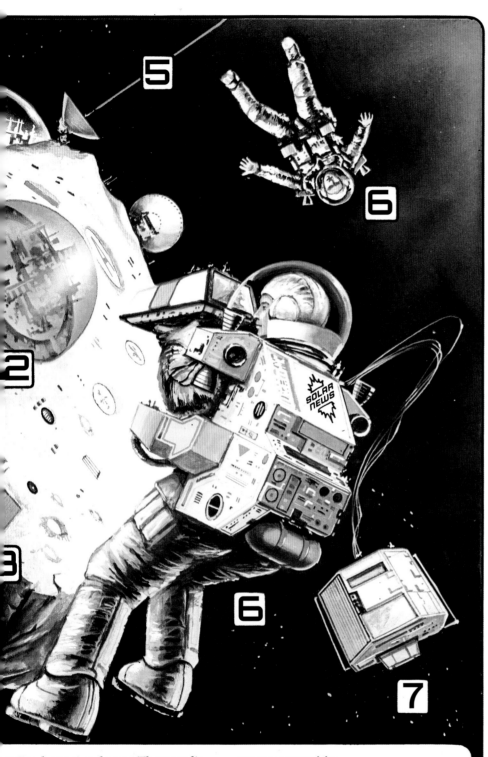

▲ This ringed world is not Saturn, but Earth in the future, according to NASA computers. Once the thousands of man-made objects in orbit start colliding with each other, a myriad of tiny particles will result and rings will form.

▲ Big corporations may pay to mine the Moon and asteroids. Professor O'Leary thinks there could be 21st century robber barons. If so, the space patrols beloved of science fiction would be necessary to head off or imprison the pirates.

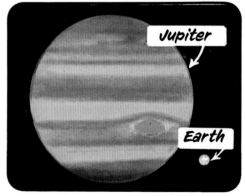

▲ The final stage in the colonization of the Solar System would be the creation of a Dyson sphere. Named after Freeman Dyson, who thought up the idea, it requires the breaking up of Jupiter – reforming the pieces into a huge Sun-surrounding shell.

*More details of the Dyson sphere on page 63

2 Food-growing domes. These are lit by sun-reflective mirrors hanging in space out of the picture. The mirrors concentrate the feeble rays of the distant Sun like magnifying glasses.
3 Radiators let excess heat out into space.
4 Some of the city's homes poke out into domes, so have a starry view.
5 Powerful laser maintains communications link with other space communities.

6 Team from Solar News making a 3-D report: Asteroid City's smelting plant is processing its first mineral lode. It is local news for other belt communities though people on the planets would be scarcely interested in such small goings-on.
7 Robot 3-D recorder monitors programme content, editing the input for instant replay.

THE NEXT 120 YEARS: A TIMECHART

What happens in the cities of the future depends a lot on what measures are taken to take care of our world, the Earth. Adequate steps must be taken to control pollution and conserve energy until oil replacements are developed and to develop the agriculture to feed 6,000 million people.

This timechart is optimistic in that it assumes such measures are taken. If they are not, the outlook is gloomy; if they are, then in 200 years mankind could conquer the entire Solar System.

1980-1990

Satellites in Earth orbit beam educational programmes to many countries in the underdeveloped Third World.

Wind turbines – modern windmill designs – are developed which can supply electricity economically.

Domestic computers run household equipment. Electronic chores include keeping accounts, ordering supplies, suggesting menus, cooking meals and keeping a diary for the people living in the house.

Newspapers supplied to homes either via a computer print-out or in electronic form over the TV screen. First domestic robots used as household 'slaves' to do simple tasks.

Terrorists steal nuclear warhead from military base. Threaten to blow up a city unless their demands are met. General realization of the appalling risks of poor security promote measures to keep atomic weapons under proper 'lock and key'.

Nuclear fuel detector-satellite placed in orbit to maintain a watchful electronic eye on the world's supplies of atomic material.

Good insulation and other energy-saving features built into all new houses.

Solar panels in general use to heat water in homes. Solar-electric cells used to generate electricity for some uses, such as recharging batteries.

World tree-planting programme begun. Aim is to restore the oxygen-producing capacity of the world's plant-life. Centuries of being chopped down have reduced the world's forest areas to a fraction of their former size. Other benefits include the production of wood-alcohol to use as a substitute for petrol in cars.

1991-2000

First major collision between satellites in orbit. Beginning of the formation of Earth's 'junkyard' ring. To slow down the development of a ring of debris, some flights are launched as 'vacuum cleaners' to remove debris.

Robots for the home improve as functions of vision, movement and handling are improved. Domestic computer runs the robot 'staff' to do most of the roles formerly done by the human housewife.

USSR launches 'cosmic greenhouse' as part of a space station complex. Air is kept breathable by plants which give out oxygen; food is obtained from fast-growing varieties of wheat, cabbage, lettuce, carrots, cucumbers, onions and other vegetables. Successful 'closed ecology' system provides valuable information for maintaining Earth's ecological balance and for the design of future space cities.

Wrist-radios developed and in general use, providing a talk-anywhere service for 24-hour emergency call system.

First deliveries of electronic mail. Hand-written letters are electronically copied, sent via a satellite-link to their destination, where the incoming message is printed out.

Electronic voting used for important decisions. System uses wrist-radios with a computer to count the votes.

3-D TV developed, using laser-holography techniques. System saves energy – people can see each other without having to travel to do so.

Burglar-alarm satellite in orbit. Provides crime prevention for large areas using sensors on the ground to detect intruders.

Water shortages in cities of developing areas. One solution, to tow icebergs from Antarctica (first proposed in the 1970s), is carried out. Operation is successful but has many unforeseen side-effects such as changing the weather in the area near the iceberg.

Sea City launched. First one is a floating airport, keeping air traffic and noise pollution away from urban areas. 'Aquaport' floats on many pyramid-shaped modules which absorb the shocks of waves and aircraft landings. Hollow modules are used for offices, shops and aircraft maintenance systems.

Underwater city built in shallow waters in the Mediterranean Sea to support mining operations there. Some people from the overcrowded land cities go there and to other undersea cities, but the vast majority prefer open skies over their heads.

Experiments made with various oil replacements for city transport, including turpentine, alcohol, liquid hydrogen and electricity.

Lunetta space mirror uses reflected sunlight to provide night-lighting in some cities.

Replicators based on the prototypes of the 1970s in general use. Shopping becomes a matter of ordering the correct chemicals from a central tank system. Despite this, the demand for hand-made craft products continues.

Solar panels in general use to heat water in homes. Solar-electric cells used to generate electricity for some uses, such as recharging batteries.

OF FUTURE CITY DEVELOPMENT

Robot systems replace many manual jobs: most in factories, many in other industries too. Growth areas with jobs for people include tourism, arts and crafts, entertainment.

2001-2050

Permanent space stations in orbit.

Uses of the mini-space cities include pollution control and medical research.

People (and robots) return to the Moon, constructing and living in a permanent Moonbase.

First Moonbaby born, signalling the start of an independent Lunar civilization.

Following a long series of experiments, it becomes possible to eliminate most hereditary defects in animals and human beings. Genetic engineering can also be used to modify the human body – increasing the lung capacity, for example, to be able to live in rarified air.

Self-contained archology constructed. Designed as one huge building, the city houses thousands of people in a pollution-free, congestion free environment. To those who dislike the idea, it seems as if the inhabitants are living in an ant-hill.

Earth's junk-yard ring system forms, despite efforts to stop it. Spacecraft have to avoid the 500-1,200 km height range because of the danger of collision with junk fragments.

Base is set up on Mars to exploit minerals.

Asteroids are used as a source of raw materials.

Work begins on the construction of a space colony for 10,000 people.

The transformation of the atmosphere of Venus begins. Oxygen producing bacteria are released from orbiting spacecraft. The aim is to reduce the high pressure and temperature of the Venusian atmosphere.

Space city for 500 people is built in orbit around Mars from materials obtained from its two satellites, Phobos and Deimos.

Wheel-shaped space hotel is built for tourists.

Lunar civilization expanding. Other Moon cities being built. Lunar mines used to provide raw materials for the construction of the space cities.

First Interplanetary Olympics held in Armstrong, the Moon's capital.

First space city, Astropolis, is completed. City exports electricity and space factory products to Earth. Most dirty industrial operations can be carried out in orbit – Earth can be left to recover from three centuries of industrial pollution.

Many sea cities drift on Earth's ocean currents. They help relieve pressures on the overcrowded land cities.

World population stabilises at 6-7,000 million people. To most people, the 'High Frontier' of space represents an escape route from an over-crowded Earth – but one that few will take. Most city dwellers do not take to the open spaces, preferring to remain in their cramped but comfortable cities, cared for by computers and robots.

2051-2099

Venus atmosphere experiments indicate that the planet can be converted into an Earthlike world.

More, and larger space cities built.

Moon civilization continues to expand.

Mars colonists consider melting the ice of the Martian poles to release more water vapour into the thin Martian atmosphere.

Space cities built in the Asteroid Belt – the beginning of an outer Solar System civilization.

BEYOND THE 22ND CENTURY

The 'Big Rain' falls on Venus. The first colonists land on the new world.

A space city is fitted with a propulsion system, allowing it to fly freely through the Solar System.

Martian poles are melted; measures result in a slightly thicker atmosphere. Genetic engineering on the colonists themselves enables them to live freely on the surface of the planet.

Man's Solar empire now consists of a newly inhabited Venus; an Earth recovering from the polluting effects of centuries of industry; cities in space; a Moon civilization; the beginnings of a Mars civilization; cities in the Asteroid Belt, various mobile space cities and thousands of spaceships crossing the void.

Work is started on the construction of a Dyson sphere – a shell to surround the Sun, making use of its energy. The material to make the shell is the planet Jupiter, which is bigger than all the other planets put together.

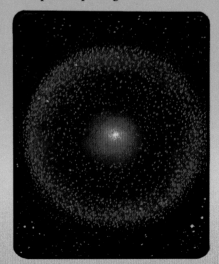

The Dyson sphere is not solid – it is a collection of worldlets. From outside the sphere, the Sun's yellow glare dims to a warm red, its light blocked off by the man-made worldlets. The red glow is caused by their warmth...

Construction of the sphere could take centuries, perhaps even 1,000 years.

Spaceships to other worlds

The craft shown in the colour picture are part of a manned expedition to another star system. The main engines, of a type not yet invented, are just cooling after a long trip from Earth. Small shuttlecraft can be seen leaving the hangar bays, their target: a new world.

In the diagram below you can see the possible target stars for the first starprobe missions of the 21st century. The stars shown are of a similar type to our own Sun. If they have planets (and astronomers cannot tell for sure at present), then perhaps life could have evolved on some of those planets as it did on Earth billions of years ago.

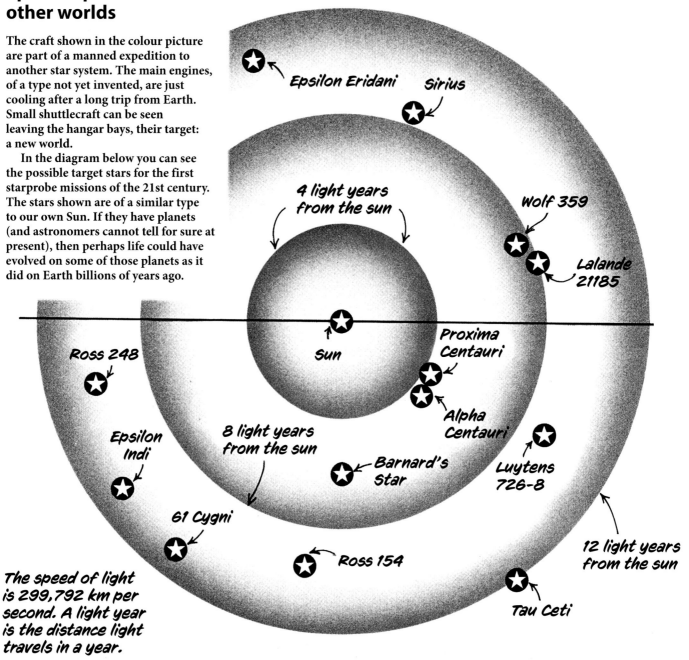

Epsilon Eridani

Sirius

4 light years from the sun

Wolf 359

Lalande 21185

Sun

Proxima Centauri

Alpha Centauri

Ross 248

Epsilon Indi

8 light years from the sun

Barnard's Star

Luytens 726-8

61 Cygni

Ross 154

12 light years from the sun

Tau Ceti

The speed of light is 299,792 km per second. A light year is the distance light travels in a year.

PART THREE
STAR TRAVEL
TRANSPORT & TECHNOLOGY INTO THE 21ST CENTURY

In the glow of an alien star

The explorers in this picture have just landed on a world orbiting a red super-giant star, a million times larger than our own Sun.

For the landing and for flight in the atmosphere, the explorers have used the streamlined ship on the left, shown balanced on its spindly-looking landing legs. The interstellar 'mother-ship', perhaps like one of the pair shown on the previous page,

remains in space, orbiting silently high above.

Blow-up plastic domes have been erected on the ground to protect delicate equipment and to give the astronauts a chance to stretch their legs. Space in the landing craft is rather cramped as it consists mainly of fuel tanks and the rocket motors necessary to fly back up to orbit.

PART THREE
STAR TRAVEL
TRANSPORT & TECHNOLOGY INTO THE 21st CENTURY

INTRODUCTION

In this last section of the book, you can find out about star travel and some of the other amazing ways of getting about which may be developed in the future.

In the last hundred years, transportation has developed from horse and steam power to the jet age and space exploration. Yet travel in and between cities here on Earth is often difficult and time-consuming. You can see some ideas – both new and not-so-new – for making day-to-day travel a pleasure instead of a torture.

Oil, the main fuel for all present-day transport systems, will run out before too long. You can read about some of the replacements which, scientists suggest, will fuel cars, trucks and planes in the 21st century.

Interplanetary exploration is now almost an everyday affair. Men have landed on the Moon and robot explorers have landed on or taken photographs of Mercury, Venus, Mars and Jupiter. When the rest of the Solar System is explored, the logical step will be to build spaceships capable of going to the stars.

Although star travel is not possible yet, you can see some of the ways in which it might be accomplished – for new worlds and new horizons, of which there are none left on Earth, will be the objectives for the explorers of tomorrow.

FROM FLOATING LOG TO SPACE SHUTTLE

For thousands of years, travelling from place to place was a slow affair. If you wanted speed on land, a horse was the fastest thing available. On the sea, a sailing vessel was the only alternative to rowing.

The steam-powered machines invented during the 1700s and 1800s made the world 'shrink' as journey times got shorter and shorter. Today you can fly around the world in a shorter time than a person of the Middle Ages would have taken to travel 200 kilometres.

In the future, there will be even quicker and, hopefully, very reliable ways of travelling as you can see in the rest of this book.

▲ The Stone-Age floating log was probably the first form of transport ever devised. The next stage in boat design was to hollow the log out to make a dug-out canoe, which could be sat in and which would not roll over as easily as a plain log.

▲ No one knows who made the first wheel, but the earliest record comes from Sumer in the Middle East. It is a sketch of funeral wagon made about 3,500 BC.

The picture above shows an Assyrian war chariot of about 850 BC. The wheels

▲ Richard Trevithick of Cornwall in England built the first steam locomotive in 1803. By the 1850s locomotives like the one above were opening up new frontiers in America, then the New World. In the USA alone, 50,000 locomotives were built between 1866 and 1900. The world speed record for steam trains is held by the Mallard. Its speed – 202 kph – has remained unchallenged for over 40 years. Today, almost all locomotives built are powered by oil or electricity.

▲ Steam power went to sea in the 1800s. The first Atlantic crossing without sail power was made by the British ship *Sirius* in 1838. The coal ran out while the ship was still at sea, so the Captain had the ship's furniture thrown into the furnace to keep the

▲ In December 1903 Wilbur and Orville Wright, who ran a bicycle business, achieved their aim of flying a heavier-than-air flying machine (balloons had been in use for a century). Orville made the first flight. After a run of 13 metres along a launching rail, the Wright Flyer rose into the air, covering 40 metres in 12 seconds. Since then, air progress has been swift and the Boeing 747 jet shown at the top right has a wingspan greater than the length of Orville's first flight. The 747 can carry up to 498 passengers with a cabin crew of 10 or more to look after them. It can cruise at nearly 1,000 kph, its wings carry 232,000 litres of fuel, and fully loaded it weighs over 350 tonnes. Even larger versions are on the way.

of chariots like this were among the first to have metal 'tyres' around their rims to make them last longer. Carts, coaches and chariots pulled by horses remained the basic means of land transportation for the next thousand years.

▲ Sailing ships are nearly as old as the wheel. By the Christian era, Roman vessels were built up to 30 metres long and could carry up to 250 tonnes of passengers and cargo. The ship above is a carrack of the 15th century. Columbus's *Santa Maria* was

a carrack, about 25 metres long with three main masts. The fastest sailing ships ever made were the clippers of the 19th century. The most famous was the *Cutty Sark* which sailed from Australia to Britain in a record 67 days.

engines going. The passenger liner *Queen Elizabeth*, shown above, was the largest (83,670 tonnes) of the ocean liners which raced across the Atlantic in this century. Now there are few passenger ships making the trip – practically everyone flies.

▲ In 1885, German engineer Karl Benz built the first car powered by a petrol engine. Early motoring was dirty, smelly and unreliable. Gradually the problems were sorted out and in 1908, the Ford Model T, the first car to be

mass-produced, was introduced. By the time production stopped in 1927, over 15 million had been made. Now there are so many cars that the congestion, pollution and accidents caused by their use are major problems world-wide.

▲ The Space Age began in 1957 when the Russians launched the first artificial satellite, Sputnik I, into orbit. Four years later Yuri Gagarin became the first man in space, and on 20 July, 1969, Neil Armstrong became the first human to

walk on another world, the Moon. The Space Shuttle, shown above, is designed to make journeys into space an everyday affair – no less than 560 missions are planned between 1980 and 1992, more than one a week.

Now read on... into the fantastic world of the future...

But before taking off into space, the first part of the book gives you a look at some earthbound transport ideas. In the main, transport of the future will be a mixture of super-high technology and a return to simple ideas, like the cheap, efficient bicycle for moving around crowded cities.

PERSONAL TRANSPORT

Short-distance travel, especially in crowded cities, is one of the biggest problems of present-day life. In the future, fuel prices are going to be higher, making short car journeys more and more expensive.

In many cities, cars are (or will be) banned anyway as the pollution and congestion they cause are too severe. In London alone, car traffic has doubled since 1970.

The ideas shown here are designed for quick, cheap and easy travel about towns.

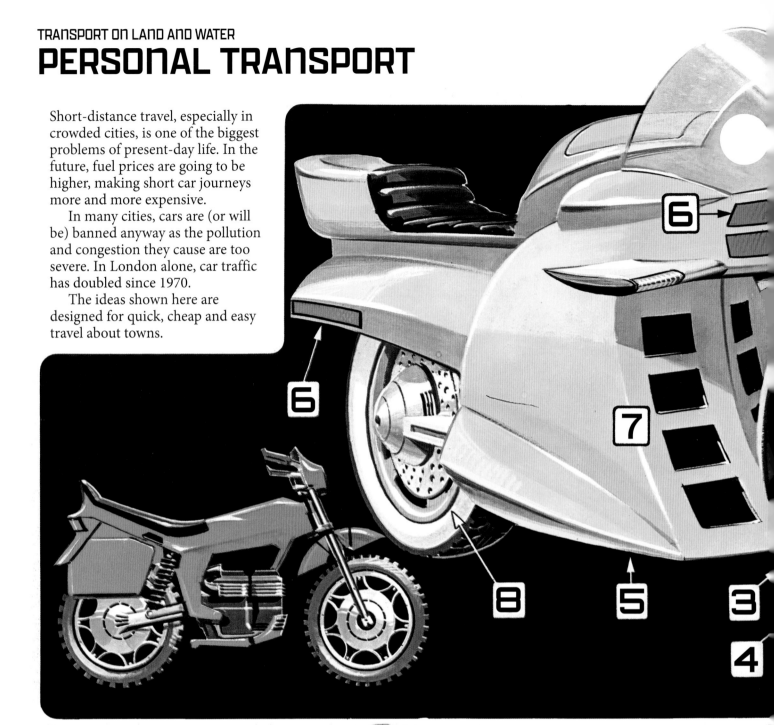

Commuting by rocketbelt

For anyone who has sat in a traffic jam or waited on a cold platform for a train, this idea, if made practical, would be a dream come true. The compressed-gas powered backpack shown was developed by Bell Aerosystems of the USA and flown in 1961. The problem was, and still is, that the fuel only lasts a few minutes. Developed versions could make traffic jams a thing of the past, though automatic radar equipment would be necessary to avoid other rocketbelt commuters!

In space, versions of the belt will be used on Space Shuttle flights, giving the astronauts perfect flight-control in the zero gravity of orbit.

Time
Road speed
Engine speed
Fuel in tank
Speed limit

9:36   136   13
4500
140

The Electronic Superbike of the Future

Motorcycles cause little or no congestion, but their biggest drawback is their poor safety record. Collisions between cars and bikes are common, and in wet weather, skids are frequent. This design, whilst looking fast and sporty, has many practical features which should be included in tomorrow's superbike. At the far left is a design from BMW for a modular motor bike. The different components can be mixed to make anything from a trail bike to a shopping bike like the one shown, equipped with big panniers to put the week's shopping in.

Both bikes have similar safety features.

1 Control panel is completely electronic, with glowing digital numbers giving all the information. This one, designed for the yellow superbike, shows the time, engine speed, road speed, the speed limit on the road the bike is on and the fuel remaining in the tank. If anything goes wrong with the unit, new components can be simply slotted in.

2 'White-wall' tyres are in fact covered in reflecting material showing the bike up at night.

3 Tyres are the run-flat type, they do not burst if punctured, allowing the motorcyclist to get home safely.

4 The disc brakes are 'cintered-steel', making them totally waterproof allowing safe braking in the wet. The brakes also have an anti-skid system.

5 Careful aerodynamic shaping of the bodywork. This protects the rider from the elements, keeps the bike firmly on the ground at speed, and improves fuel consumption, as less power is required for good speeds.

6 Large glow-lights front and rear help pick out the bike day and night.

7 The engine is a Wankel rotary. At present this type of engine is not perfected but it shows huge potential. The shopping bike could be electric – refuelled by plugging into the mains supply at night.

8 Wheels are made of injection-moulded foamed-nylon. Lighter than metal ones, they do not rust and are cheap to make.

And if you want to keep fit ...

The bicycle is likely to be one of the major transport systems in tomorrow's towns. It is cheap, easy to park and provides healthy exercise. The important thing is to develop networks of cycle-ways to separate bikes from cars and trucks.

This Steyr-Puch design is a prototype for tomorrow's bicycle. It weighs just 8.61kg, thanks to its sail-shaped frame which is made of aluminium and plastic. The bike has no separate tyre pump – its seat support can be moved up and down to do the pumping. The bar at the back includes a large rear lamp and indicator blinkers. Basic power for them is a standard battery, but it is recharged using a mini solar-cell on top of the unit.

Blinker unit →

CARS AND TRUCKS

Petrol is going to get more and more expensive as supplies dwindle in the future, so energy-saving design will be the theme for cars and trucks for the rest of this century.

By the 1990s, electric cars should be developed sufficiently to make them a good alternative to petrol-engined ones.

In the 21st century, many scientists think that liquid hydrogen (LH_2) will be used as the basic fuel for most vehicles including aircraft. Although LH_2 needs careful storing and requires big fuel tanks, it is clean and non-polluting.

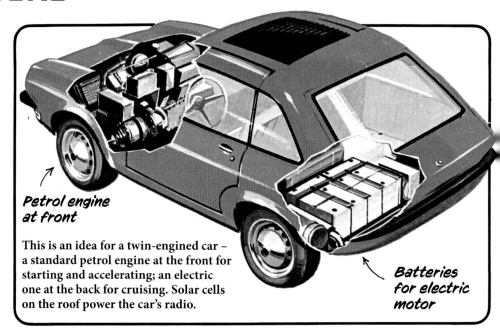

Petrol engine at front

Batteries for electric motor

This is an idea for a twin-engined car – a standard petrol engine at the front for starting and accelerating; an electric one at the back for cruising. Solar cells on the roof power the car's radio.

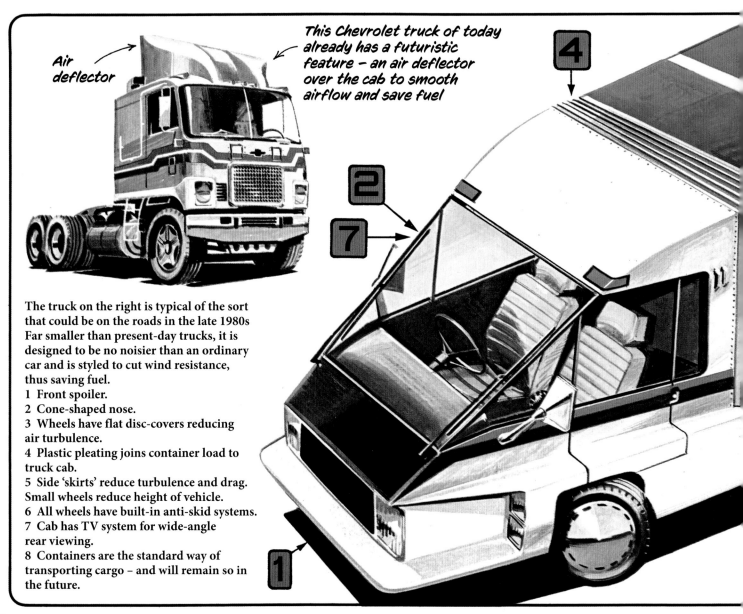

Air deflector

This Chevrolet truck of today already has a futuristic feature – an air deflector over the cab to smooth airflow and save fuel

The truck on the right is typical of the sort that could be on the roads in the late 1980s Far smaller than present-day trucks, it is designed to be no noisier than an ordinary car and is styled to cut wind resistance, thus saving fuel.

1 Front spoiler.

2 Cone-shaped nose.

3 Wheels have flat disc-covers reducing air turbulence.

4 Plastic pleating joins container load to truck cab.

5 Side 'skirts' reduce turbulence and drag. Small wheels reduce height of vehicle.

6 All wheels have built-in anti-skid systems.

7 Cab has TV system for wide-angle rear viewing.

8 Containers are the standard way of transporting cargo – and will remain so in the future.

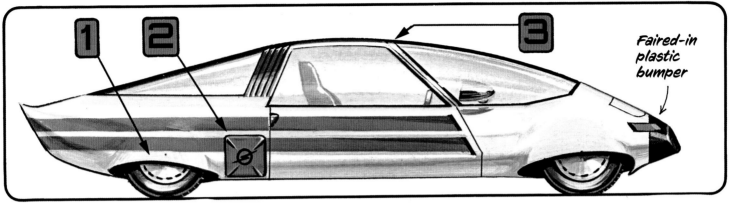

Faired-in plastic bumper

This streamlined electric car has lots of interesting features including covered-over wheels to cut down on air drag (1). It is powered by electric motors. The battery is in module form (2) being quickly replaced at any 'filling station'. For overnight stops, it could be recharged by plugging into the mains supply. The roof has solar cells (3) built-in to power small systems like radio tape-player and the automatic navigation system. The car is largely made of aluminium and other lightweight materials. Styling is done in the wind tunnel to cut drag and so improve fuel (in this case, electricity) consumption. Even petrol-engined cars should be fairly economical to run. Designers are even now working on cars which will run over 20 km on a litre of fuel.

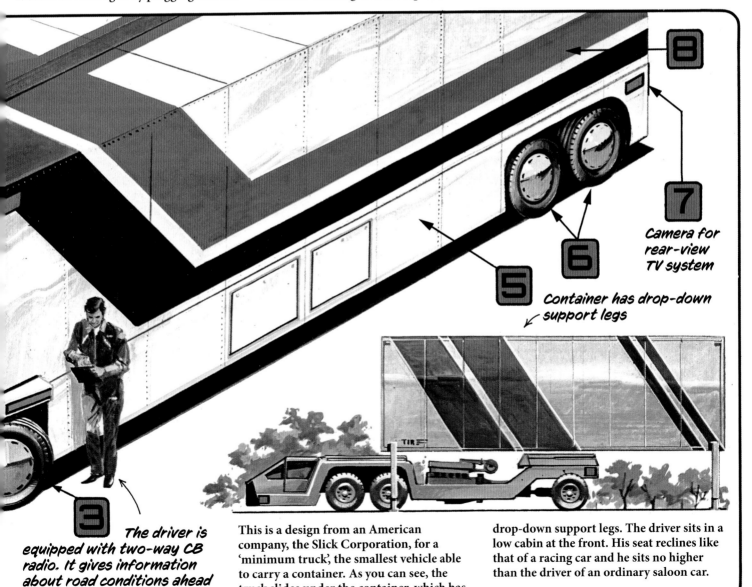

Camera for rear-view TV system

Container has drop-down support legs

The driver is equipped with two-way CB radio. It gives information about road conditions ahead

This is a design from an American company, the Slick Corporation, for a 'minimum truck', the smallest vehicle able to carry a container. As you can see, the truck slides under the container, which has drop-down support legs. The driver sits in a low cabin at the front. His seat reclines like that of a racing car and he sits no higher than the driver of an ordinary saloon car.

TOMORROW'S TRAINS

Although most passenger train services in today's world lose money, they still have several advantages over other transport systems. They are very safe, and can take loads from city centre to city centre causing little pollution and no congestion.

Freight services, which already carry 70% of the world's inland freight, are likely to carry still more – few people wish to see the number of juggernaut trucks increasing in the future.

Most trains in the rest of this century will be electric powered. The train below is a futuristic solution to the problem of long-distance travel across the world.

An old-fashioned answer to a problem of tomorrow – coal power

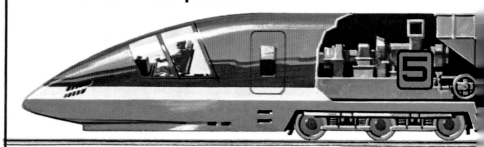

The 'fluid-bed' furnace is one solution to the problem of powering tomorrow's trains. In a fluid-bed furnace, crushed coal (1) is fed into a sand-filled firebox (2), while jets of scorching hot air (3) vibrate and support the sand/coal mixture. Burning coal in this way is very efficient, giving off little or no pollution and generating great heat.

Water contained in a boiler (4) is heated.

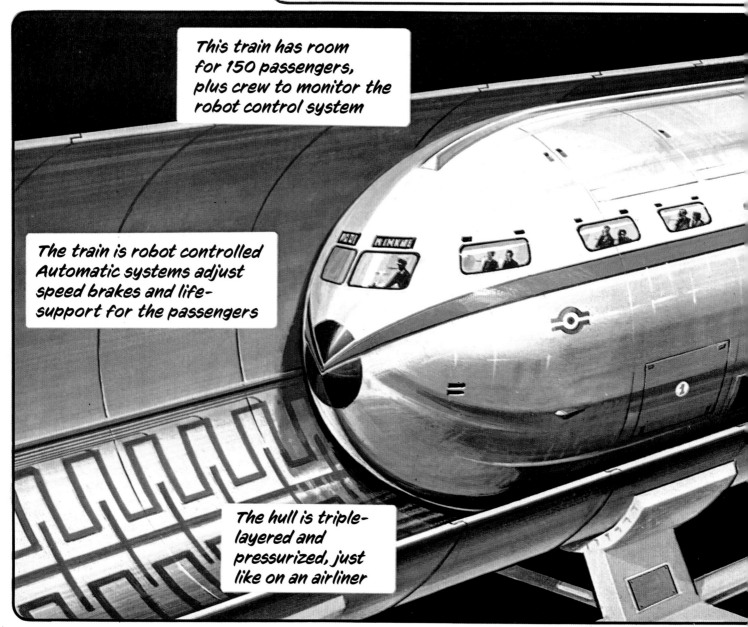

This train has room for 150 passengers, plus crew to monitor the robot control system

The train is robot controlled Automatic systems adjust speed brakes and life-support for the passengers

The hull is triple-layered and pressurized, just like on an airliner

The steam rushes along pipes to spin turbines (5). The spinning turbines power electric motors (6), one to each axle. The steam is condensed back into water after it has spun the turbines so there is no need to carry large quantities of water.

An alternative to carrying the furnace on the train is to have central fluid-bed power stations, each feeding electricity to an overhead pick-up line system like the one used on many of today's railways.

Whichever system is used, the outlook for coal as a power source is bright – experts estimate that the world's coal supplies will not run out for 1,000 years.

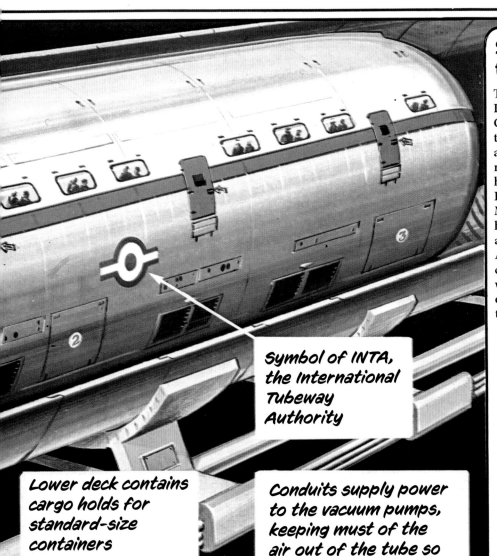

Symbol of INTA, the International Tubeway Authority

Lower deck contains cargo holds for standard-size containers

Conduits supply power to the vacuum pumps, keeping must of the air out of the tube so the train has a friction-free ride

Supertube under the ground

This bullet-shaped train, proposed by Dr Robert Salter of the American Rand Corporation, is what some scientists think will replace high-speed passenger aircraft in the future. The train would run through underground tunnels, hundreds of metres below the ground. It would be supported by MAGLEV Magnetic Levitation (just like two horseshoe magnets repelling each other) and would be propelled by electric motors. A maximum speed of over 13,000 kph could be achieved because the tunnel would have practically all the air pumped out of it, so there would be no air pressure to act as a barrier to the train's progress.

↖ Friction heats fuselage and wings

Tube train remains ↗ cold in vacuum tube

▲ Concorde's wings and nose heat up by hundreds of degrees during supersonic flight, due to the friction of the air that has to be forced out of the way. The tube train's fuselage remains icy-cold as it hurtles through its vacuum tunnel.

UNDER AND OVER THE WAVES

Transport on and in the water will be designed to help tap the almost untouched mineral riches under the seas and to provide world navies with more efficient defence systems.

Mining minerals underwater will be a big growth industry in the late 20th century. Already oil rigs operate in the North Sea. In the warmer waters of the Red Sea in the Middle East, mining operations are already underway to extract the rich veins of minerals under its sea bottom. In the future these operations will extend into deeper waters. Even the Antarctic will be an area of mining operations in the 21st century, as all Earth is plundered for minerals.

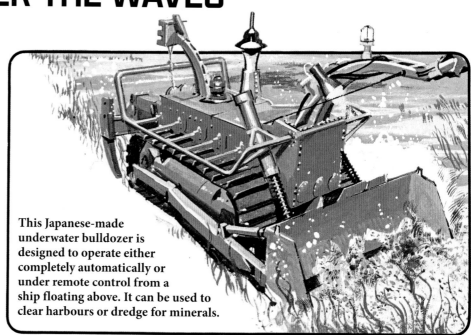

This Japanese-made underwater bulldozer is designed to operate either completely automatically or under remote control from a ship floating above. It can be used to clear harbours or dredge for minerals.

▲ In the crystal-clear waters of the Caribbean Sea, tourist submarines will operate giving holiday makers splendid views of fish and plant life under the waves. The submarine above is based on a German design of the 1970s. It can carry 14 passengers plus crew. Submarines like this could act as 'buses' to transport people to the underwater cities which may be built in shallow waters across the world.

▲ Submarines equipped with nuclear missiles could be out of date by the year 2000. Latest spy-satellite equipment shows that it may be possible to detect submarines underwater, so they will no longer be able to cruise in secrecy.

▲ This picture shows a robot loading dock of the year 2000. A cargo submarine is being loaded with containers by automatic machinery, ready for transporting across the world. One big advantage of travelling underwater is that there are no storms to battle through and no waves to slow the ship down. But many of the world's shipping lanes are very shallow: a big supertanker travelling through the English Channel, for instance, has only a few metres between the bottom of its hull and the sea bed. A submarine would not be able to submerge in waters like this – it would have to ride on the surface like all the other vessels.

▲ This picture shows an all-too-likely scene of the near future. A group of terrorists have successfully planted explosives in an oil rig. A fast patrol hydrofoil has fired an anti-shipping missile at the terrorists' boat – only to have it destroyed by an anti-missile missile fired by the terrorists. In the sky, two helium rig-patrol blimps cruise in – one to help fight the fire, one to try and sink the terrorists.

▲ Hydrofoil patrol boats are fast but small; they cannot carry much fuel so have quite a short range. Mid-ocean refuelling could be carried out by submarine using an aircraft-style probe and drogue system as shown above.

▲ This 200 kph craft could revolutionise naval warfare. It is an SES – a Surface Effect Ship. Its two sidewalls run in the water but flaps on bow and stern capture an air bubble to keep most of the hull out of the water. Water-jets would squirt the vessel along at high speed. The SES shown above is a mini aircraft carrier on top and a cargo carrier underneath. In this case the cargo consists of hovercraft troop carriers for amphibious beach assaults. A commercial version of the SES could fill the speed gap between fast aircraft and slow ships. It could run fully loaded from Europe to the USA in about 30 hours, several times quicker than an ordinary cargo vessel.

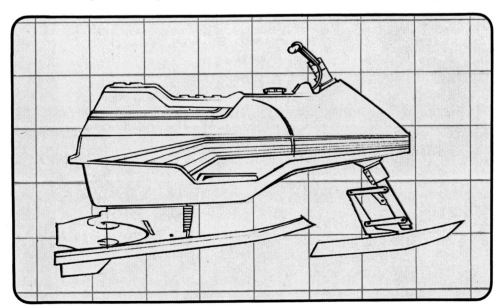

Aqua-ski marines

The Kawasaki Wet-Bike, already in production, skates along on twin skis. Powered by a motorbike engine, the Wet-Bike can whizz along at 40 kph. If the rider falls off, the Wet-Bike's engine stops and it floats nearby ready for reboarding.

Developed versions would be an ideal mount for marines to ride in amphibious attacks. They could be used in river patrol work too – the draught of the Wet-Bike is only a few inches and it causes little wash, so river banks and bottoms would remain undisturbed by its passing.

JUMBOS, SSTs AND AIRSHIPS

Air transport has hit a plateau in the 1970s – big improvements in speed, size and range are technically possible but too expensive in practice.

'SSTs', or 'SuperSonic Transportation' vehicles such as Concorde, are a typical example of technical brilliance but bought at too high a price.

Aircraft now being developed for flight in the 1980s and '90s, such as the Boeing 757 and the Airbus A3l0, are designed to use less fuel than current types. They include detail improvements and new materials such as super-strong carbon-fibres, but look little different from jetliners which have been flying since the 1960s.

Really high-speed flight will probably be more easily achieved using spacecraft or tubetrains like the one on page 74 which, by 2050, could be competing successfully for some long-haul airliner business.

▲ Curious fin-like wing extensions on aircraft wings provide more lift for slower landings and reduced drag for faster and more economical cruising. The multiple 'sail' immediately above is based on the feather structure of a bird, the Marsh Harrier. The first production aircraft with tip extensions, in this case simple fins, is the American Longhorn business jet. Detail improvements like this are going to be a feature of aircraft throughout the 1980s.

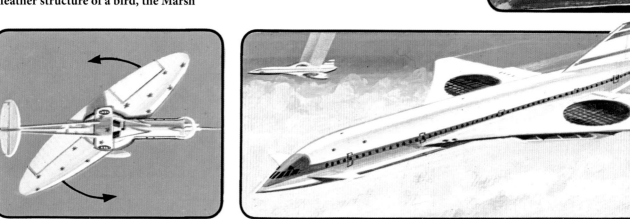

▲ This odd craft has a wing which sweeps from straight out for landing, to swept-back-and-forward for high speed flight. Experts think it will be a good system as it needs only one heavy pivot point for the oval-shaped wing.

▲ This airliner could use the power from satellite-borne laser beams to heat air in wing ducts. The superheated air would rush out of nozzles in the rear of the wing to propel the airliner forward. Computer systems on board the satellite would track the airliner, keeping the lasers aimed at the wing heater panels. The aircraft would only need to carry small reserve engines and sufficient fuel to make an emergency landing if the laser beams were cut off.

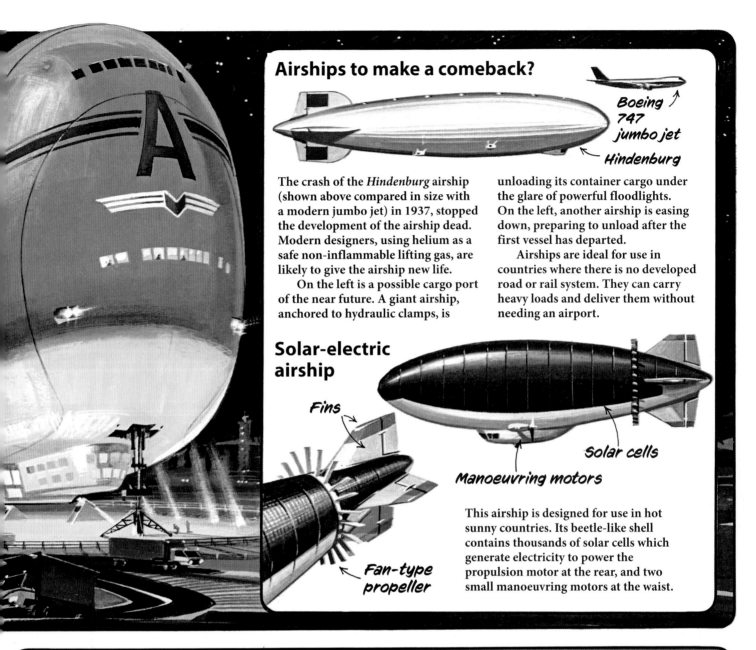

Airships to make a comeback?

Boeing 747 jumbo jet

Hindenburg

The crash of the *Hindenburg* airship (shown above compared in size with a modern jumbo jet) in 1937, stopped the development of the airship dead. Modern designers, using helium as a safe non-inflammable lifting gas, are likely to give the airship new life.

On the left is a possible cargo port of the near future. A giant airship, anchored to hydraulic clamps, is unloading its container cargo under the glare of powerful floodlights. On the left, another airship is easing down, preparing to unload after the first vessel has departed.

Airships are ideal for use in countries where there is no developed road or rail system. They can carry heavy loads and deliver them without needing an airport.

Solar-electric airship

Fins

Solar cells

Manoeuvring motors

Fan-type propeller

This airship is designed for use in hot sunny countries. Its beetle-like shell contains thousands of solar cells which generate electricity to power the propulsion motor at the rear, and two small manoeuvring motors at the waist.

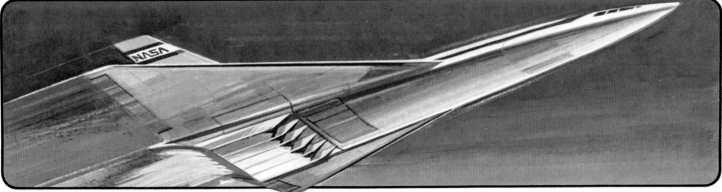

▲ Airliners powered by liquid hydrogen – LH$_2$ – could be common in the petroleum-short 21st century. This design typical of the studies being made on future aircraft by major aircraft manufacturers, could fly 500 passengers at three times the speed of sound. It would fly so high that (in theory) its supersonic boom would have dissipated to little more than a mild thud by the time it got to ground level. LH$_2$ is a good substitute for petroleum-based fuel, but it takes up more fuel-tank space and needs very careful storage. It is plentiful, being obtained from water, which is not (yet!) in short supply. Current airliner designs could be converted to use LH$_2$ by hanging large fuel tanks from their wings or under their fuselage.

THE SPACE SHUTTLE

The Space Shuttle is the world's first re-usable spacecraft, designed to take off vertically like a rocket, manoeuvrc in orbit like a spaceship, then fly home like a glider.

Because the orbiter section can be re-used up to 100 times, unlike ordinary rockets which crash to destruction with each space shot, the cost of flight into space will be greatly reduced. In everyday terms though, prices are high – customers will pay from $10,000 to more than $21 million for cargo space.

Its American designers believe that the Space Shuttle and craft like it will become as vital to our future as ships and aircraft are today, and that experiments undertaken in orbiting Shuttles will lead to advances that will affect every man, woman and child.

Spaceplane to orbit

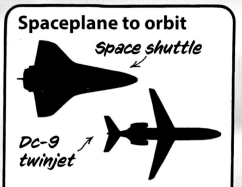

Space shuttle

Dc-9 twinjet

Shuttle orbiter, to the same scale as a modern jetliner. It has an overall length of 37.l m and a wing span of 23.8 m.

Spaceplane is covered with 34,000 heat resistant tiles to protect the craft from the fiery heat of re-entry

Delta wings enable the shuttle orbiter to land back on a normal runway

The shuttle can take heavy loads into space – a maximum of 29,484 Kg. Its designers are already thinking about bigger versions.

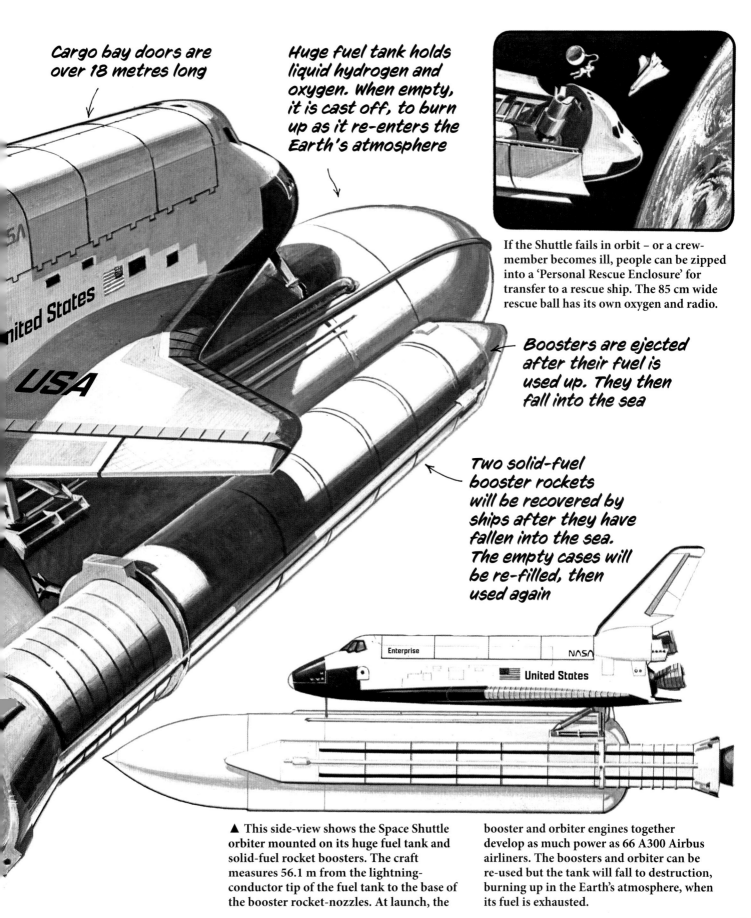

Cargo bay doors are over 18 metres long

Huge fuel tank holds liquid hydrogen and oxygen. When empty, it is cast off, to burn up as it re-enters the Earth's atmosphere

nited States

USA

If the Shuttle fails in orbit – or a crew-member becomes ill, people can be zipped into a 'Personal Rescue Enclosure' for transfer to a rescue ship. The 85 cm wide rescue ball has its own oxygen and radio.

Boosters are ejected after their fuel is used up. They then fall into the sea

Two solid-fuel booster rockets will be recovered by ships after they have fallen into the sea. The empty cases will be re-filled, then used again

Enterprise   NASA   United States

▲ This side-view shows the Space Shuttle orbiter mounted on its huge fuel tank and solid-fuel rocket boosters. The craft measures 56.1 m from the lightning-conductor tip of the fuel tank to the base of the booster rocket-nozzles. At launch, the booster and orbiter engines together develop as much power as 66 A300 Airbus airliners. The boosters and orbiter can be re-used but the tank will fall to destruction, burning up in the Earth's atmosphere, when its fuel is exhausted.

JOURNEY INTO SPACE

By the mid 1980s, flights by Space Shuttle should be an everyday affair.

Loads for the huge cargo hold of the Shuttle, 18.3 metres long, will be many and varied. At present, planned cargoes include the ESA Space lab for research work; the Grumman Aerospace beambuilder, a robot designed to manufacture girders for space stations; the Space Telescope, and dozens of different types of satellite.

Flights will leave from Kennedy Space Center at Cape Canaveral in Florida or from Vandenberg Air Force Base in California; a typical mission will last anything from seven days to nearly a whole month.

▲ On the launch pad stands the complete Space Shuttle system, consisting of the winged orbiter connected to a huge fuel tank. Either side of the tank are two solid-fuel rocket boosters. The whole lot weighs over 2,000 tonnes. When rockets and three motors of the orbiter all fire together. All five motors develop a thrust of over 3 million kg to push the Space Shuttle off the launch pad into space.

▲ The orbiter's two orbital manoeuvring engines thrust it into orbit at a speed of 28,300 kph and a height of 185 km. By using the orbital manoeuvring engines the orbital height can be varied between 161 and 966 km. The picture above shows the orbiter, cargo doors open, displaying a typical load – the ESA Spacelab. In this, four scientists can work in shirtsleeves on research experiments such as processing medicines or producing ultra-pure metals and glass.

The scientists aboard the orbiter will need to be healthy, but not superhuman – the Space Shuttle is designed to give a smooth take-off and landing. Maximum acceleration should be no more than 3G – three times the force of gravity. Early space flights subjected astronauts to 9G or more.

▲ As the speed builds up, the orbiter's wings generate lift just like those of an aircraft. The motors of the booster rockets have to swivel to offset this, otherwise the craft would pull over into a loop and crash down to the ground.

▲ The craft accelerates skywards and when it is 46 km up the two booster rockets separate. Small thruster rockets push them away from the fuel tank. They will splash down into the ocean to be recovered by ships waiting for them.

▲ Still with its main engines on, the orbiter climbs, drawing its fuel from the huge tank. It casts off the tank just before it arrives in orbit. The tank will be destroyed as it falls back through the Earth's atmosphere.

▲ The Space Telescope will be a typical Shuttle load. An orbiting telescope like this should make it possible to examine stars which are 100 times fainter than those seen by the most powerful telescopes on Earth.

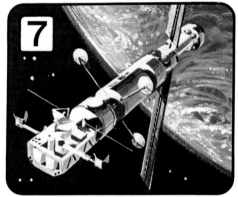

▲ Small space stations like this could be constructed by linking several Spacelabs together. Solar cell 'wings' would power the station. Plans are also being discussed to use the big fuel tank as the basis of a space station, perhaps the first of many.

During their stay in orbit, anything from a week to a month, crew and scientists will have many of the comforts of home, including a wide variety of food, washing facilities and a specially designed zero-g lavatory.

▲ After its mission is completed the orbiter glides back to Earth. During re-entry through the atmosphere, the nose and leading edges of the wings glow dull red with the heat generated by smashing into the atmosphere at 26,765 kph. Almost

as useful as the loads it can take up are the loads (up to 11,340 kg) it can return to Earth. A damaged satellite, for example, can be brought back for repair, then taken into orbit again.

EXPLORLING THE SOLAR SYSTEM

Unmanned spacecraft will continue to explore the Solar System. Some, like the one on the right, are already in space. Others, like the comet-chaser shown opposite, could be launched by the Space Shuttle in the mid 1980s.

Eventually, manned spaceships will be launched from space cities orbiting the Earth. They will be pure 'Space' ships, not streamlined and unable to fly through the atmospheres of other worlds. Small shuttlecraft carried in cargo bays will carry astronauts from orbit to the surface of the planet they are exploring.

Craft like the one below might be plying the spaceways throughout most of the next century.

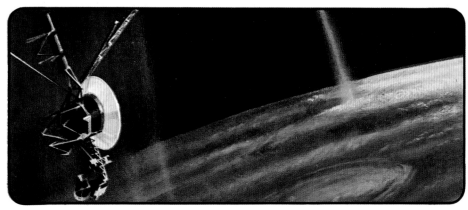

▲ This picture shows *Voyager I* as it passes through the 'flux tube of Io'. Io is a satellite of Jupiter, the flux tube a region of intense magnetic disturbance between satellite and planet. Future Shuttle-launched missions include the Solar-polar voyages. Two craft will fly above and below the Sun's north and south poles, regions which are unexplored. Scientists hope to learn more about cosmic rays, and solar conditions which cause weather changes back on Earth.

The mobile mini-planet

This curious-looking spaceship, based on the ideas of Dr Krafft Ehricke, is designed for long journeys through the Solar System. Its pencil-like spine contains nuclear-fusion powerplants to energise the propulsion system, laser drilling and communication equipment, life-support and other power needs. The 'wings' are like skyscraper blocks, containing living quarters. The craft spins, providing simulated 'gravity' in the wings by centrifugal force.

Dawn on Titan, moon of Saturn

In this picture you can see explorers, who have landed in a shuttlecraft from their orbiting 'mother ship', collecting samples of Titan's air, soil and rocks.

Titan, largest moon of Saturn (seen high in the sky in the picture), is about 5,800 km across – much bigger than Earth's Moon. Titan has an atmosphere of methane, hydrogen and other gases. Clouds of a strange orange colour have been observed, but their exact nature is, at present, unknown. Titan may have the conditions in which complex molecules may accumulate. On Earth, such molecules evolved into primitive lifeforms, so Titan is an extremely important place for scientists to study – there may be life on other worlds after all. If it exists on Titan, it will be very unfamiliar though – conditions are very different from those on Earth and evolution could create strange solutions to the problem of living on a world whose average temperature is about -150°C.

Saturn

Earth

Titan

★ *Three worlds shown to the same scale*

▲ In 1986, Halley's comet will make its closest approach to Earth in 76 years. The ion-engined craft above has been proposed by the American Jet Propulsion Laboratory to fly by the comet. It would then zero in on the nucleus of another comet, named Tempel. Another possible target for the 1980s is comet Encke, which nears the Sun every 3.3 years. The wings of the craft contain solar-cells to power the ion-engines. Early versions of these power plants were placed in Earth-orbit in 1969 during the SERT (Space Electric Rocket Test) programme. Seven years later they were still in working order, a necessity for the long mission times planned for craft using them in the future.

STARPROBE 'DAEDALUS'

A journey to the stars, once thought to be fantasy, will be possible within a century according to a study called Project *Daedalus* carried out by the British Interplanetary Society.

The starprobe is named after the legendary Greek who made wax wings to escape from a Mediterranean island. His son, Icarus, flew too near the Sun. His wings melted and he crashed. Daedalus, shown in the 1493 woodcut above, was successful.

Starship *Daedalus* is designed to be powered by nuclear 'bomblets' which would accelerate it to a staggering 3,869 km per second. Its destination – Barnard's Star, six light years from the Sun.

▲ Construction of *Daedalus* is carried out in orbit around Callisto, a satellite of the planet Jupiter. Fuel for the ship, a chemical called Helium-3, could be mined from the atmosphere of Callisto or even that of Jupiter itself. *Daedalus* is huge and weighs as much as a small ocean liner. Building the star probe would take several years using mainly automated assembly machines under computer control. In the picture above, the two stages of the probe are ready to be joined together.

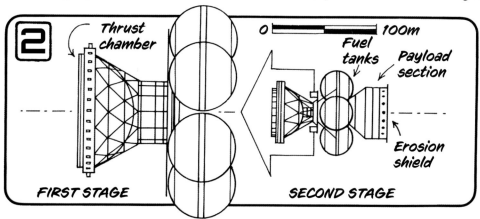

▲ This side-view shows some of the ship's design features. It is fuelled by nuclear pellets. These are injected, 250 per second, into the thrust chamber. A ring of electron beams compresses each pellet to cause a nuclear fusion explosion. The reaction thrusts the ship on its way. When the second stage takes over, a similar but smaller system is used. At the front of the ship, ahead of the payload section, is a shield designed to protect the craft from erosion from interstellar gas and dust.

▲ *Daedalus* blasts off on its journey to Barnard's Star, nearly six light years from the Solar System. Astronomers think the star has at least one, and perhaps several planets orbiting it. The first stage accelerates the ship to 900 km per second.

▲ *Daedalus* is equipped with mobile robots called wardens to maintain and, if necessary, repair parts of the ship during the half-century journey. They can also repair each other if any damage or malfunctions occur.

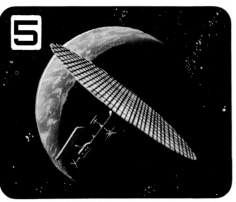

▲ Contact with *Daedalus* is maintained using a vast three-km-wide radio telescope in orbit around the Earth. The array is made of hundreds of small telescopes, linked to a computer to form a super-powerful unit.

▲ As *Daedalus* approaches Barnard's Star, its collision protection system is deployed. This is nothing but a dust cloud ahead of the ship, but because of its high speed any object hitting it will be instantly vapourised.

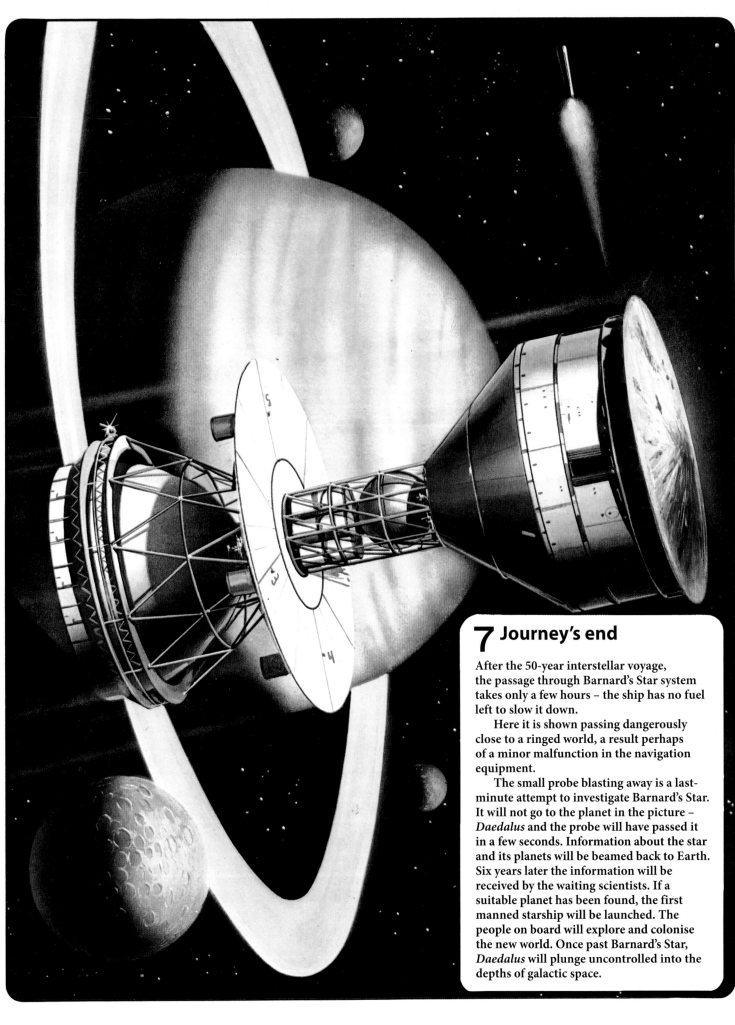

7 Journey's end

After the 50-year interstellar voyage, the passage through Barnard's Star system takes only a few hours – the ship has no fuel left to slow it down.

Here it is shown passing dangerously close to a ringed world, a result perhaps of a minor malfunction in the navigation equipment.

The small probe blasting away is a last-minute attempt to investigate Barnard's Star. It will not go to the planet in the picture – *Daedalus* and the probe will have passed it in a few seconds. Information about the star and its planets will be beamed back to Earth. Six years later the information will be received by the waiting scientists. If a suitable planet has been found, the first manned starship will be launched. The people on board will explore and colonise the new world. Once past Barnard's Star, *Daedalus* will plunge uncontrolled into the depths of galactic space.

BY ASTEROID TO NEW WORLDS

If the *Daedalus* starprobe reports that a habitable world has been found, the next step could be the construction of a manned starship. The one shown here uses as its structure an asteroid, one of the millions of rocks orbiting between Mars and Jupiter.

Even though it uses ready-made material, its construction would be extremely complex and would take a long time.

The starship is an indication of the gradual expansion of the human race we might expect in the centuries to come. In the future, the 20th century will be seen as a major turning point in history – the point at which mankind took the first steps off Earth.

▲ This idea for hollowing out an asteroid is based on a method suggested by science fiction writer Larry Niven. Other science fiction ideas have come true – perhaps this one will too. Astronauts start by landing on a suitable roid (future slang for asteroid), drilling into its centre with super-powerful lasers. Water tanks are placed in the middle, the drill hole sealed up and the roid made to spin like a pig on a spit, using ion-drive engines mounted on its equator.

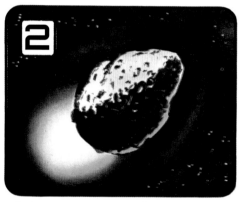

▲ A giant space mirror focusses intense solar heat onto the spinning roid, slowly melting it. When the water in the centre boils, the expanding steam blows up the roid like a giant balloon. Calculations will have to be precise for success!

▲ After the roid has cooled, robots and astronauts landscape the interior, in this case designed to resemble the countryside of 'Old Earth'. Spacelocks allow shuttles to enter and leave the roid, now christened *Ark II*.

▲ Before *Ark II* starts its journey, ecological engineers like the one above check the internal environment. *Ark II* has been made to spin and the resulting centrifugal force plants the engineer's feet firmly on the 'ground' – which is the inside of the roid's skin. After testing, *Ark II's* environment will be shut down and darkened until it nears the target star system. The crew of *Ark II* is not human – the flight will be controlled by robots and computers.

5 The start of a fantastic voyage

Here you can see *Ark II* picking up speed under the power of its nuclear motors. The accompanying ships are making final external checks. If they do not keep clear, *Ark II's* exhaust beam will vapourise them. *Ark II* is aiming at Saturn to make a 'sling-shot' past it, using its gravity pull to boost the ship's speed out of the Solar System.

The humans on board *Ark II* are carried as 'seeds' – fertilised ova – in suspended animation. Animals, fish and birds are carried in the same way. When *Ark II* nears the target, robots will activate the seeds, raising them as 'test-tube babies', educating them on board the Ark for their life on the new world.

On the journey; passengers are protected from space radiation by the thick rocky crust of the Ark. Engines, observation posts, communications equipment and computer banks are all built into galleries surrounding the huge central living area.

STAR TRAVELLERS

Even the nearest star is so far from the Solar System that its light takes over four years – travelling at over 300,000 km per second – to get here.

Daedalus-type probes would take nearly half a century for the journey. According to Einstein's Theory of Relativity, it is impossible to travel as fast as light, which would be necessary to cut the journey to a reasonable time. So either people must be content to take centuries to reach their destinations or scientists must discover as-yet-unknown laws of nature to take a 'short-cut' across the Universe. Perhaps it could be a 'space-warp' in which a starship would disappear from one part of the Universe only to reappear in another.

One thing is fairly certain – if space-warps or something like them exist, scientists will discover and make use of them sooner or later.

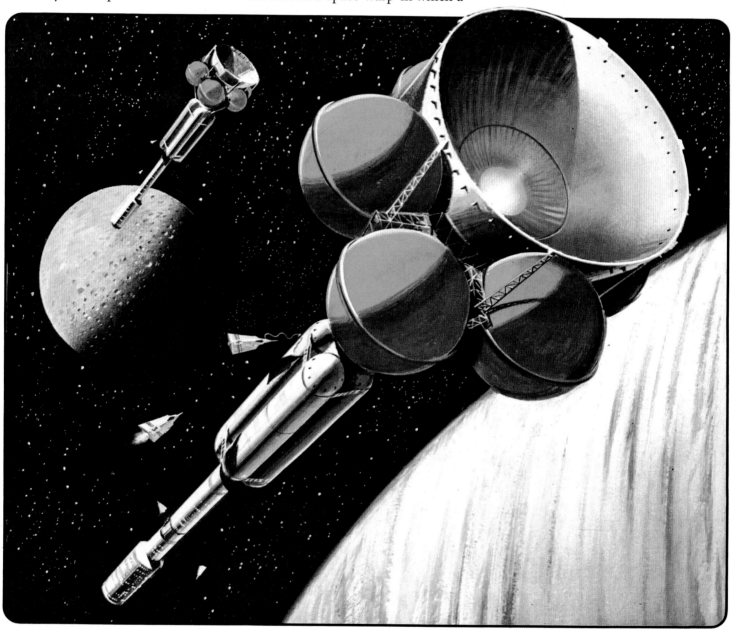

▲ These starships are shown parked in orbit round the Jupiter-type world of another star. The vessels are being refuelled by scoopships, which dip into the planet's atmosphere, gathering chemicals and gases suitable for the starships' engines.

The operation is monitored by an 'artificial intelligence', a super-computer aboard each starship. They have controlled the huge ships throughout their journey. The human crews have been in a deep sleep, induced by an artificial hibernation process, waiting to be woken from their centuries-long slumber by their robot captains.

Starships like this could slowly cross the galaxy, searching for habitable worlds and alien beings. The human crew could be woken at each stop, decide on the course of action to be taken, then go back into hibernation until the next target star is reached. The journey would be a one-way trip in time for them – if they ever returned to Earth, they'd discover their families and friends would be long dead.

▲ Some scientists have suggested that 'black holes', tiny super-dense remnants of stars, may be gateways to other parts of the Universe. According to one theory, a starship entering a rotating black hole would reappear through a 'white hole' far away in space, defeating Einstein's law that nothing can travel faster than light. In the picture above, a starship, the *Galactica*, has made such a journey and is shown approaching a space terminal in a distant part of the galaxy. The ghostly lights hanging in space are 3-D laser-images designed, like runway lights of today, to guide the craft in to a safe landing. On the right, control officers in charge of approach and landing systems watch the *Galactica* from their pressurised pod.

▲ Future travellers check their arrival data with a robot clerk. Their journey has not been by starship, but by teleportation. They are, in fact, not 'real' people, but copies involved in a fantastic process, the reconstruction of living matter. Back on Earth, computers made detailed examinations of their atomic structure. This was put into code and the data transmitted across space using laser beams. At Starport Central, computers receiving the information used vats of the necessary chemicals to reconstruct the travellers in their original images.

Horrifying though this idea may sound, a laser-copying process already exists to make images of inanimate objects.

ACROSS THE UNIVERSE

If interstellar travel becomes commonplace – and that is a big 'if' – what sights could star travellers of the far future see? On these pages you can join a starcruise organised by ITC, the Interstellar Tour Company.

The design of the starship is totally fictitious: no one has designed such a craft yet. As shown here, its rear section contains engines for manoeuvring within planetary systems. The arrow-nose contains living quarters, navigation equipment and as-yet-unknown machinery to drive the ship from star to star at super-speeds – essential if the tourists wish to return to their homes within their lifetimes.

Witnessing starbirth...

Stars are formed within nebulae – vast clouds of gas and dust in the depths of space. As the gas and dust collects, it gradually heats up until eventually a star shines out, fuelled by the fusion energy of hydrogen.

First port of call for the ITC tour is such a nebula. This one is called M16, and it lies nearly 6,000 light years from the Solar System. Young, hot stars can be seen glowing through the misty veils of the nebula.

The square hatch in the kilometre-long starship contains shuttle craft to ferry passengers down to the surface of any strange world the ship comes near.

...and stardeath

Here, the starship is silhouetted against the glare of a giant star whose matter is being drawn out in a vast spiral by the titanic gravitational pull of its tiny partner star, a black hole.

A black hole is the ultimate death for a star. As a star runs out of its hydrogen 'fuel', it explodes, throwing its outer layers off into space. The remaining matter collapses in upon itself, getting smaller and smaller and denser and denser. Eventually it is so small and so dense that even light cannot escape its gravitational pull – it winks out of existence, becoming a black hole.

The glow you can see at the end of the spiral is not the hole, but X-rays given off by the giant star's matter as it is sucked in. The starship would need to keep well clear, otherwise it would be destroyed.

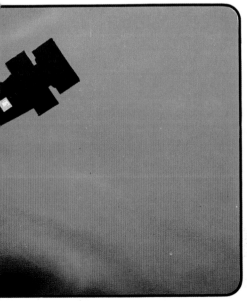

Outside the galaxy

A final, and spectacular, view before the ITC tourists return home – our own galaxy, the Milky Way, viewed from a point some 300,000 light years above its centre. The position of the Solar System is marked with an arrow, though from this distance it would be completely invisible except through a very powerful telescope.

You can see the Milky Way any clear night on Earth – it is the misty band extending across the sky. Its huge (100,000 light years across) spiral is formed of 100,000 million stars. The Milky Way is one of many galaxies – there are billions of others scattered like grains of sand across the Universe.

Early this century, spaceflight was regarded as just a dream.

As late as 1957, Britain's Astronomer Royal dismissed it as 'utter bilge'. Unfortunately for his reputation, the Russians launched Sputnik I a few months later and the Space Age began.

Star travel is at present as much a dream as the idea of satellites in orbit once was. But if it is possible at all, one day within the next century the first starship will travel through interstellar space.

1980-1990

USA launches NASA Space Shuttle into Earth orbit from Cape Canaveral, Florida.

USSR launches 'Kosmolyot' (spaceplane) which looks like a smaller Space Shuttle. It is designed to carry cosmonauts to and from Russian space stations.

Space lab made in Europe flies into orbit in the cargo hold of the Space Shuttle. A mixture of astronauts and scientists are the crew for this and other missions.

First American woman astronaut flies aboard the Space Shuttle.

Safe airships using non-inflammable helium lifting gas are used for cargo and passengers transport in Brazil and Peru. Other designs are used in Africa and South-East Asia.

USSR builds wheel-less hovertrain. It is powered by a linear electric motor. The train runs on a metal track, suspended just above it by a magnetic field, at speeds up to 800 kph. Train has the advantages of ordinary railways, such as all-weather and low-cost operation, together with the speed of an aircraft.

Research capsule from *Galileo* spacecraft enters the atmosphere of Jupiter in 1984.

Automatic navigator for cars in general use. Using a mini-computer aboard car and sensor equipment on the road, it gives the driver route instructions, computes fuel consumption, and so on.

Spacecraft using an ion-drive engine flies to intercept and photograph Halley's Comet, 1986.

Passenger aircraft fly powered by engines which use very little fuel.

Two spacecraft are launched to fly far above and below the Sun – a region so far totally unexplored.

Voyager spacecraft passes Uranus in 1986, Neptune in 1989. Eventually leaves the Solar System to pass into the depths of interstellar space.

1991-2000

Experimental civil airliners fly using liquid hydrogen as a fuel instead of petroleum-based kerosene.

Electric cars in general use. Batteries better than current types power them. They can be recharged from the mains supply overnight or exchanged at a 'filling station'.

High-speed hydrofoil gunboats in general use by world navies.

Helium-filled airships used for city-to-city transport. Quiet turbo engines assist in take-off and landing.

2001-2050

Passenger module

space shuttle

Passenger-carrying shuttle craft carry tourists into orbit.

Improved rockets, replacing the Space Shuttle, come into operation.

First human beings land on Mars.

Manned expeditions travel to most parts of the Solar System, including the asteroids and the moons of Saturn.

Experimental aircraft fly using satellite-based laser beams to power them.

Huge 'clipper ships' equipped with solar sail shuttle cargo between worlds. The ships are driven by the weak but continuous pressure of sunlight on the kilometers-wide sails.

First high-speed underground vacuum-tunnel train developed. First route runs across the USA.

2051-2100

Scientists achieve the complete conversion of matter to energy – theoretically the most powerful source of power available.

Vacuum-tunnel trains replace aircraft on some long-distance routes across the world.

Mining of Helium-3 from the atmospheres of Callisto and Jupiter.

Helium-3 and deuterium processed into fuel pellets for use in *Daedalus* starprobe being built in orbit around Callisto.

Starprobe completed, using parts made in space factories orbiting Earth, Mars and Callisto.

Starprobe departs on its 50-year journey to Barnard's Star.

Last of petroleum fuel used up on Earth. Replacement fuels like liquid hydrogen, coal and solar energy now power the transport system of the world.

2101-2150

Starprobe *Daedalus* arrives at target star. Information from the probe received by scientists in the Solar System about six years later (Barnard's Star is about six light years from the Sun).

Information received indicates that *Daedalus* has discovered a suitable planet for colonization.

Other starprobes launched at different target stars; first manned starship construction starts, using a small asteroid as a basis.

First manned asteroid-starship leaves the Solar System.

THE FAR FUTURE

Teleportation developed. A computer breaks down the atomic structure of an object into a code system which is transmitted at the speed of light to the target point. There another computer reconstructs the object.

'Space warp' achieved. Objects can be made to apparently vanish from one point, only to reappear in another. System developed to be used on board starships.

Explorers aboard early starships arrive at their target worlds, only to find people waiting to greet them. The reception committees have travelled virtually instantly by space-warp equipped starships.

Human civilization slowly spreads through the galaxy.

INDEX
ROBOTS

FUTURE CITIES

STAR TRAVEL

GLOSSARY

ALIEN Stranger or foreigner. In this book, the word refers to creatures from other planets.

APOLLO Spaceship that took astronauts to the Moon between 1969 and 1972.

ASTEROID BELT Thousands of rocks, verying in size from a pinhead to hundreds of kilometres across, orbiting in space mainly between Mars and Jupiter.

BLOOD CLOTTING Thickening of blood that happens when the skin is cut. As the blood solidifies, it seals the cut.

CARBON FIBRE Very light, very strong material used at present in, for example, the fan blades of some jet engines.

CB SET Citizens' Band radio. Used, especially in the USA, by car and truck drivers to talk to each other from inside their vehicles, swapping information on road conditions.

COMET Comets are balls of ice, dust and rock, drifting in huge orbits around the Sun. Some develop tails milions of kilometres long as they near the Sun. The tails are long streamers of gas, resulting from frozen gases boiling from the heat of the Sun.

GALAXY Giant cluster of stars. Our own galaxy, the Milky Way, contains about 100,000 million stars.

HELIUM Gas used in modern airships. Unlike hydrogen it will not catch fire.

HYDROFOIL Ship with underwater wings, called foils, which raise the hull out of the water at speed.

INDUSTRIAL REVOLUTION Period in the 18th and 19th centuries during which powered machinery started to replace human and animal muscle power.

INTERSTELLAR The space between the stars. The word comes from the Latin 'inter' – between, and 'stella' – star.

ION DRIVE System of powering spacecraft using electrically charged particles to provide thrust.

LASER Intense beam of light, used for a variety of purposes, such as cutting, welding and as a replacement for some types of radio communication.

MICROWAVE A form of radio wave. Can be used as a power beam – a receiving antenna converts the energy in the beam to electricity.

MODULAR Device made up of various parts, modules, which fasten together. The different modules can be easily changed or rearranged.

MONORAIL Train which runs on one rail instead of two.

POLLUTION Literally, waste in the wrong place, causing unforeseen side effects, usually hazardous to health.

SENSOR Device to 'sense', or gather information about its surroundings.

SOLAR CELL Flat pane of silicon material which converts the energy in light to electricity.

SOLAR PANEL Glass-fronted black panel, mounted to face the Sun. The Sun's heat warms water flowing through tubes inside the panel.

SPEED OF LIGHT Just under 300,000 kilometres a second. A light year is the distance light travels in a year.

WANKEL ROTARY ENGINE Type of engine in which, unlike an ordinary car engine where the pistons move up and down, a triangular piston spins round in a chamber.

ZERO-G Weightlessness, as felt in deep space or in orbit.

Computer counting answer

The word is JAB. It has been programmed into binary using the system 1 = A, 2 = B, and so on. People can use different coding systems (called programmes) depending on the problem they are working on.

CREDITS

Written by
Kenneth Gatland and David Jefferis
Designed and produced by
David Jefferis Limited
Illustrated by
Gordon Davies
Terry Hadler
Brian Lewis
Michael Roffe
George Thompson

The cover was painted by the late Brian Lewis, a brilliant artist who is greatly missed.

Acknowledgements
We wish to thank the following individuals and organizations for their assistance.
Astronautics and Aeronautics magazine
Bell Aerospace
Boeing Aerospace Corporation
British Interplanetary Society
Arthur C. Clarke
Cosanti
Energy Equipment Ltd
European Space Agency
Future magazine
Grumman Aerospace
Heron Suzuki (GB) Ltd
Joint European Torus project
JPL Jet Propulsion Laboratory
Kawasaki Motorcycles Ltd
Lockheed Aerospace
McDonnell Douglas Aerospace
NASA
Omni magazine
Omtec Replication (for the 3-D copies described in 'Computers in the home').
Popular Mechanics magazine
Puch bicycles
Rockwell Aerospace
Slick Corporation
Spaceflight magazine
TRW Inc